What P vs. problem?

Ramaswami Mohandoss

ISBN:978-0-9989746-1-3
(Orange Window Publishing)

DEDICATION

To my dad, the first mathematician I met in my life.
To my mom, the first innovator I met in my life.

BY THE SAME AUTHOR

In Few Words

Let us derive $e=mc^2$

CONTENTS

1. INTRODUCTION

In 2011, SpaceX announced something extraordinary and even revolutionary—a reusable rocket system. Back then, for most of us, the thought of a rocket returning to the earth from its orbit and, more importantly, making a vertical landing was beyond imagination. Elon Musk, the founder of SpaceX, had mentioned that a reusable rocket system is crucial in our mission to conquer Mars. A few years later, in 2015, SpaceX created history. Their orbital rocket's first stage made a triumphant return and a vertical landing for the first time. In the subsequent years, SpaceX made tremendous breakthroughs improving its success rate and accuracy. As of June 6, 2019, SpaceX had attempted forty-seven landings of its first stage rockets on a solid surface and succeeded on forty occasions. SpaceX continued to improve upon its landing accuracy too. While SpaceX's initial landings were ten kilometers in the planned target location's vicinity, it improved to less than ten meters in the next few years. Truly remarkable, right?

Now let us take a scenario back on earth. Let us say you place an order for a product from an e-commerce website. The product gets shipped, and one fine morning, you are informed that it has arrived at the local delivery center, ready to be delivered on the same day. Though the product is close to you, maybe less than a few miles away, the logistics company will find it impossible to predict the exact delivery time in a way that is both optimal and cost-effective for them. Wait! We can pinpoint the precise location of a reusable rocket's landing, but are we likely to wait at the doorstep for the entire day to receive a package that we know for sure is in the vicinity? Yes, that is the exciting thing about this world where *some of the most challenging problems look deceptively simple on the surface.* We don't have a solution for some genuine problems yet. If we delve deeper into understanding what makes them hard, the path will lead us to the ultimate question $Does\ P = NP?$ (also called the $P\ vs.NP\ Problem$)

Apart from being one of the biggest mysteries in Computer Science and whose solution could fetch you a million US dollars[1], it ($P\ vs.NP\ Problem$) also has a philosophical connection. This book is not an attempt to solve the problem but to capture the journey to discover the problem. That path was not a trivial one. Mathematicians and Computer Scientists formulated numerous concepts on the way. Some of those concepts are not intuitive in the first read and may sound confusing to many. But that's what makes Computer Science a fascinating field to explore.

Our pursuit in the following 150 odd pages would be to discover the problem ourselves. We shall build the required intuition and knowledge brick by brick through every chapter. While we go through all the critical theories, we shall focus on grasping the various ideas and concepts by performing thought experiments and solving multiple problems. We would also work out all the required math needed to get the concepts through the course. Though not mandatory, basic programming knowledge will help grasp the

---

[1] As of 2021, P vs. NP problem is one of the seven prize problems (also called millennial problems) identified by Clay Mathematics Institution. A reward of one million US dollars is allocated to the solution of each of the seven problems.

intuition in a single read. In the footnote section of every chapter, I shall be providing details of the books, or articles of any kind, that I had to refer to while preparing the content.

The *P vs. NP Problem* is often represented through the following Venn diagram. In summary, we intend to discover and understand every bit of the detail captured in this diagram through the following chapters.

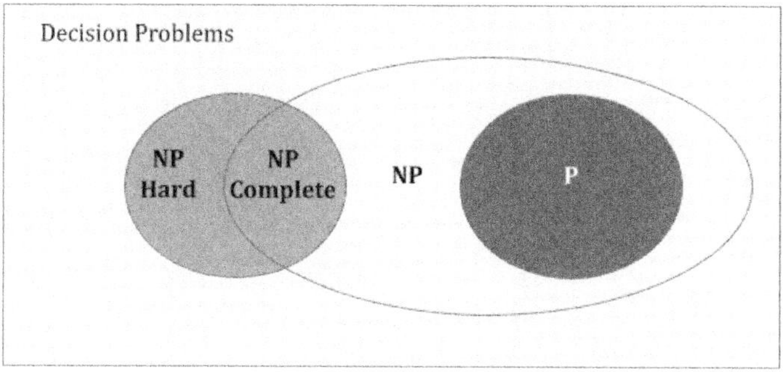

Figure 1

So, let us get started. We shall begin our pursuit from that point in time in history that initiated an important debate.

2. THE BEGINNING

2.1 Could we know everything?

Do we know everything about this world? A reasonable person is likely to answer this *No.* A far more difficult question to answer would be, *Could we know everything?* In other words, are humans capable of knowing everything? Some believed in that possibility, i.e., *Yes, humans can know everything,* and one such individual was David Hilbert. In the nineteenth century, David Hilbert was a German mathematician and an influential person. He firmly believed that we could arrive at a theory that would explain everything about this world through mathematics. He spent his lifetime trying to prove this, and despite being challenged by several other mathematicians and philosophers, this belief stayed with him till the very end. The epitaph in his tombstone reads—*We must know. We shall know.* Those were the famous lines he spoke after his retirement address. The above statement was Hilbert's response to the Latin maxim: *Ignoramus et ignorabimus* or *We do not know, we shall not know.*

To begin understanding the $P\ vs. NP\ Problem$, we should learn about an important program that Hilbert formulated and pursued during the end of the nineteenth and the beginning of the twentieth century. *Hilbert's Program* attempted to clarify and solve some foundational crises that mathematics faced then.

What were those foundational crises?

Since the days of Plato and Aristotle, philosophers worldwide have tried to make sense of the world through mathematical equations. Many of them succeeded in their pursuits, and here are some crucial moments from history. Long back, Pythagoras captured the fundamental relationship in Euclidean Geometry in a right-angled triangle. Sir Issac Newton laid the foundation for Classical mechanics through his laws of motion. Albert Einstein was able to unify the theories of conservation of mass and energy in a simple equation: $e=mc^2$. Our chaotic world is explained beautifully by the following equation: $x_{t+1}=kx_t(1-x_t)$.

In essence, philosophers and scholars believed mathematics could help us see the objective truth. If mathematics can help us see the objective truth, some mathematicians (Hilbert included) thought it should be possible to arrive at a framework within mathematics that would help us describe the world (read *completeness*). They also believed that applying that framework should not lead to contradictions and paradoxes (read *consistency*).

Unfortunately, the frameworks that existed back then were neither complete nor consistent. Cracks started to emerge with the discovery of paradoxes, and one of the most famous paradoxes is Russell's paradox, discovered by Bertrand Russell.

In 1901, Bertrand Russell, a British Mathematician, discovered a paradox in set theory that poked holes into the foundations of mathematics. Here is the intuition of the paradox through the analogy of a barber.

Let us consider a village where the administration mandates every person clean-shaven. One barber in the town shaves all those, and those only, who do not shave (themselves). Let us consider two sets:

> P: The set that includes every member of the village
> B: The set that consists of the village barber who shaves all those, and those only, who do not shave (themselves)

Now, the question is—*Who shaves the barber?*

If you think about it carefully, for the barber to shave his beard, he shouldn't have shaved it himself. If he hadn't shaved it himself, he would cease to be a barber because, as a barber, he is expected to shave anyone who does not shave, and that would include himself. The barber seems to both shave and not shave his beard, and this contradiction is the essence of Russell's paradox.

Russell's paradox strengthened the doubt about whether mathematics can help us reason the world. Russell was able to identify this paradox because the framework and the rules (naive set theory in this case) were not rigorous enough. For instance, in Russell's paradox, set B's informal definition failed to capture who the barber is. Hilbert took up the challenge and proposed formulating a more robust framework through his program.

In the new framework, Hilbert proposed writing every mathematical statement using precise *formal language*. In other words, we would not informally make a mathematical statement using a language like English. Hilbert intended to avoid ambiguity and assumptions seeping into the framework through formal language.

Here are some examples of informal statements and their formal equivalents:

- Informal: 2 and 4 add up to 6. Formal: $2 + 4 = 6$
- Informal: The square root of 16 is 4. Formal: $\sqrt{16} = 4$
- Informal: Either cats or dogs. Formal: cats $\vee$ dogs ($\vee$ corresponds to Boolean OR)

The formal language would include a finite set of foundational axioms that would be true. An axiom could be as simple as—for any two variables a and b, a + b = b + a. The formal language would also include well-defined rules that we would use to manipulate the axioms. In the above example, the rule applied is +, i.e., addition.

Second, Hilbert pursued to prove the completeness of the framework. As part of the framework, he intended to include mathematical proof that would show that one can logically derive any mathematical statement (that is true) through the foundational axioms and the formal language.

Third, Hilbert wanted to show that the framework is consistent. Again, as part of the framework, he intended to include mathematical proof that would show that one would never reach a contradiction or a paradox by applying the formal language on the axioms.

Finally, he wanted the framework to include a *computation method* for deciding the truth or falsity of any mathematical statement and to show that the framework is decidable.

Hilbert believed that the foundations of mathematics would be intact if he succeeded in establishing such a framework. To summarize, the framework would need to include the following:

1. A formal language that consists of a set of axioms and well-defined rules
2. Proof for completeness
3. Proof for consistency
4. A computation method for deciding the truth or falsity of any mathematical statement

Many mathematicians and logicians were skeptical about Hilbert's approach and believed his goals were impossible to achieve. One such mathematician was Alan Turing from Cambridge. Twenty-two-year-old Alan Turing proved Hilbert wrong through his path-breaking paper in 1935 and demonstrated it differently from his peers. It was that difference that laid the foundation for modern computing.

2.2 The Challenge

Before moving forward, now would be the right time to define the following category of problems: *decision problems*. In computation theory, a problem is considered a decision problem that can be posed as a "Yes/No" or "True/False" question. Here are some examples of decision problems.

- Is 2 the square root of 4?
- Is the number 11 a prime number?

Coming back to Hilbert's program, we learned that Hilbert intended to formulate a framework in Mathematics that would be complete, consistent, decidable, and also include a formal language with a set of well-defined axioms and rules. In essence, we could use that framework to explain everything about the world. Many mathematicians contested Hilbert's theory and proved him wrong.

Turing's target on Hilbert's program was unique. He challenged the decidability aspect of the program. As we recall, to prove that the framework is decidable, Hilbert had stated that his framework would include a computation method that would decide on the truth or the falsity of every mathematical statement. Also, Hilbert was vague and hadn't clearly defined what a computation method is. Though the notion of an *algorithm* was yet to be clearly defined back then, Hilbert was informally referring to an algorithm by computation method. If you observe, in his pursuit of formulating a framework that would be decidable, Hilbert had made a crucial assumption. He had assumed that a computation method existed that would decide the truth or the falsity of any mathematical statement.

In other words, Hilbert assumed that an algorithm existed that would help decide on any decision problem because checking the truth or falsity of a mathematical statement is a decision problem, and Hilbert intended his framework to explain everything. It is this assumption that Turing challenged, and Turing was convinced that Hilbert's perspective of computation is incorrect. Turing had reasons to believe (which will soon be clear) that solutions to specific decision problems don't exist and are beyond the reach of the human mind.

Did Turing succeed in his pursuit? Of course, he did, and we know that from history. But how did he do it?

To prove Hilbert's assumption wrong, Turing had to clarify what computation is and, more importantly, formally define an algorithm. Hilbert was not specific to either of them. In that pursuit, Turing chose first to design a *mathematical model of a computer.* He intended the model to solve any decision problem as long as one can express its computation method (or solution method) through a sequence of steps, interpretable by the model. These steps thus become the algorithm to solve the problem. Through that model, Turing pursued to show that we will not be able to write an algorithm for some decision problems. In the following two chapters, we shall build intuition and delve into the details of the model, its interpretable steps, and what it means to write an algorithm for solving a decision problem. In other words, we will begin learning how Turing drew on paper the design of what we call today the modern computer.

2.3 A Computer on Paper

Remember, we are in the early years of the twentieth century and are still theorizing the concept of computers. When Turing wrote his paper in 1935, the word *computer* would typically refer to a human who would do computational tasks. When a machine did something similar, it was called a *digital computer*. In this chapter, we shall build the intuition for the various aspects Turing considered essential to define the computer's theoretical or mathematical model (aka model). In the next chapter, we shall go about formalizing the same. Turing pursued a model that would be simple and adequate. A simple model will seamlessly scale as the size of the problem increases. We consider a model adequate when it has all the necessary aspects to solve problems of varying complexities. In this chapter, we shall arrive at those aspects through a thought experiment.

Our thought experiment would involve designing a *palindrome solver*. In other words, it is about solving the following decision problem—whether an English word is a palindrome? A word is a palindrome if it reads the same way from both ends. In the English alphabet, examples include words such as *madam* and *anna*. In a language enumerated from the binary alphabet (0 and 1), 10101 and 111 are examples of a palindrome. We shall call words formed through combinations of 0's and 1's as binary strings going forward, and we shall only focus on binary strings for our thought experiment. The idea is, if our model can solve this problem for a binary string, it is a matter of scaling and configuring the model to extend to the English alphabet. After all, we can represent every letter in the English alphabet through ASCII encoding as a binary string. Remember, the pursuit is to arrive at a simple and adequate model. Now, how would we know if a string is a palindrome?

10101

While the task of identifying a palindrome might look trivial, i.e., one can recognize that through a glance, what is that exact mental process we go through in that glance? Our thought experiment would involve dissecting that. To make it easier for our thought experiment, let us consider a slight variation of the decision problem—How would we know if a string is a palindrome when blindfolded? Yes, we will be performing the thought experiment keeping our eyes closed. You might wonder why we should do this, but it will help us dissect our exact mental process. Just hang in there, and the rationale will be evident in a few moments.

As part of the model, we would need a medium to help us feel the word and solve the problem blindfolded. In our example, we can consider the medium a thin strip of paper with enough space to hold a long word or a sentence with multiple words. We can visualize the strip of paper to be divided into independent cells. Each cell has a fixed real estate to hold one letter. We would recognize the value in a cell through touch and feel.

								1	0	1	0	1							

The second aspect we would need is the alphabet. In our example, the alphabet consists of letters 1 and 0. Remember, the medium is a strip of paper long enough to hold a sentence to print the above string, i.e., 10101. We would leave the remaining cells blank on a tape with more than five cells. So, blank is a special symbol that we need to consider as part of the alphabet. We shall use a special symbol ƀ to represent a cell that does not have a letter.

ƀ	ƀ	ƀ	ƀ	ƀ	ƀ	ƀ	ƀ	1	0	1	0	1	ƀ	ƀ	ƀ	ƀ	ƀ	ƀ	ƀ

Once we have the medium and the alphabet, the third aspect is the set of operations. The operations would involve either moving from one cell to the other (in either direction) or reading and interpreting what is available in a specific cell, i.e., the ability to interpret a 0, 1, and a blank space.

To summarize, so far, we have identified the following aspects to be part of the model:

1. A thin strip of paper where we can print our string.
2. The string can have letters from the binary alphabet, i.e., 0 or 1, and the special symbol ƀ.
3. A set of well-defined operations that would include the following abilities:

a. To interpret the letter (including a blank) present in a cell.
b. To move to the next cell (left or right)—we shall do this through touch and feel.

With the above, what is the technique that we can adopt? You could pause and think through before you move ahead. We have provided one possible method below:

1. Lay the strip of paper on a table.
2. Using the index fingers of both of your hands, start interpreting what is there in each cell from either end of the tape.
3. Suppose you find a blank cell under the right index finger—Move your right index finger to the next cell on the left. Similarly, if you find a blank cell under the left index finger, move your left index finger to the next cell on the right.
4. Repeat the above step until you either have a 0 or a 1 under your left and right index fingers. In other words, repeat the previous step until you get both the ends of the string under your left and right index fingers.
5. If the letters under both of your index fingers are different, we can exit, deciding that the string is not a palindrome. If the two letters are the same, you could simultaneously move both your index fingers to read the next cell, i.e., move your right index finger to the cell on the left and the left index finger to read the cell on the right. Figure 2.3.1 gives a pictorial view of this technique.

6. Repeat the previous step until both the fingers meet. If both of our fingers touch, it means that we have converged, and we can decide that the word is a palindrome.

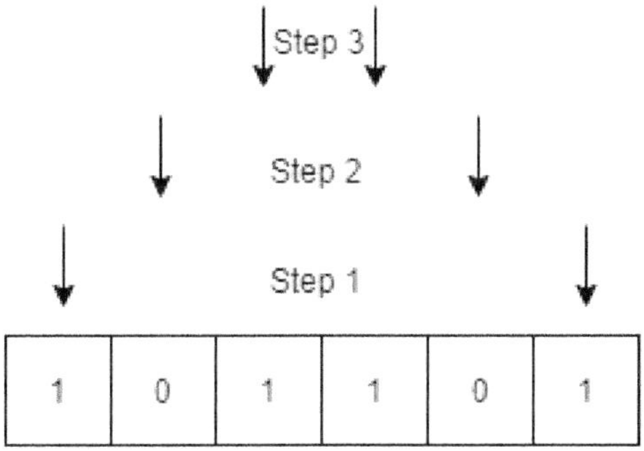

Figure 2.3.1

The above technique is fair, but it does have its limitations. Of course, it is limited to how much we can stretch our hands, and the input string has to fit within that. Can there be a better way? Remember, we are still blindfolded. We can feel the letters in the strip of paper, but we cannot see them. Let us try considering a new aspect—let us say we have access to some additional tools, i.e., a special pencil and an eraser to change the letter present in a specific cell. Using these tools, we can change a cell's value to any other letter that belongs to the alphabet. In essence, we are adding another kind of operation to overwrite the value in a specific cell. Now, would that allow us to arrive at a better technique? Before that, let us consolidate the aspects that we have collated so far.

Here is our evolved set of aspects for the model:

1. A thin strip of paper where we can print our string.
2. The string can have letters from the binary alphabet, i.e., 0 or 1, and the special symbol ƀ.
3. A set of well-defined operations that would include the following abilities:
    a. To interpret the letter (including a blank) present in a cell.
    b. To move to the next cell (left or right).
    c. To update the value of a specific cell.

With the new aspect added to the list, let us explore a different technique. Instead of two hands, we shall now try with only one hand. The difference with this technique is that we would not feel and interpret two letters simultaneously. Instead, we would interpret and remember the first letter before reaching out to the last letter to verify it is the same as what we remember. This technique would also involve erasing the cell whose value we choose to either remember or verify. Figure 2.3.2 gives a pictorial view of this new technique.

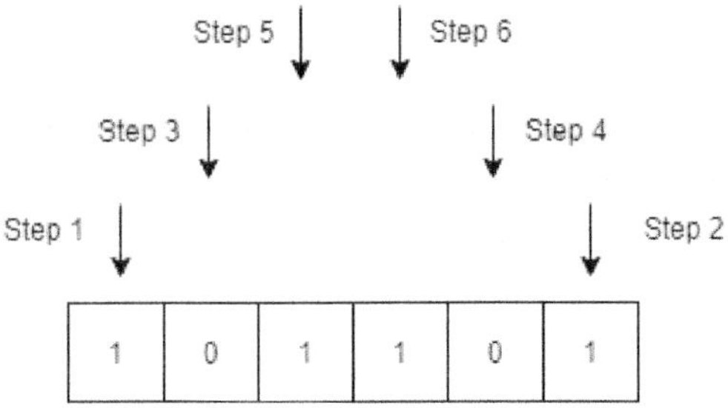

Figure 2.3.2

A high-level outline of the steps involved in this technique is provided below.

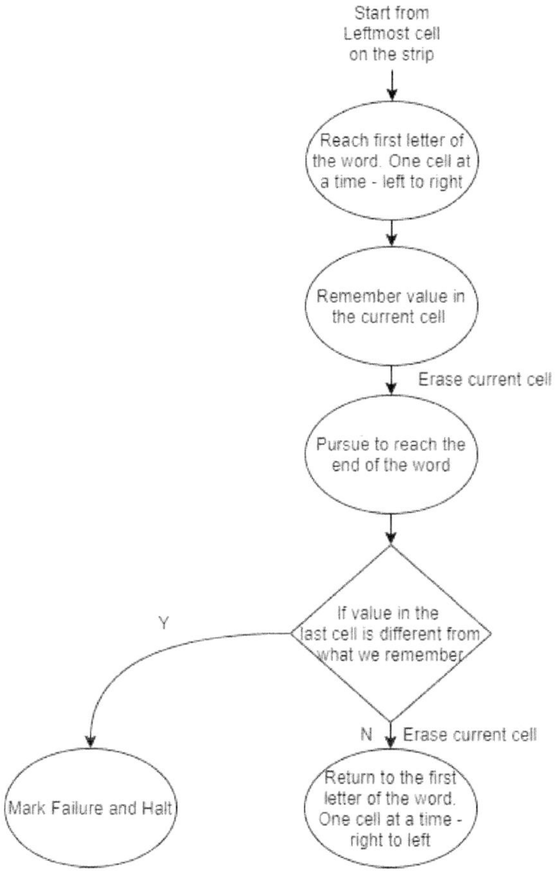

Figure 2.3.3 [Step 1]

While the above flowchart outlines the technique, it requires certain refinements. In the following few pages, we shall refine the method as much as possible. We shall add every imaginable detail to the flowchart to perform these steps mechanically for any word. Here is the first set of refinements.

1. The above steps would apply to a pair of letters in the word, and we would need to iterate until we either reach a failure step or end up erasing all the letters in the word. In other words, we would need to loop through the steps mentioned in Figure 2.3.3.
2. Also, the technique will differ (only slightly) from the above when the word's length is odd. The steps mentioned in flowchart 2.3.3 are for words of even length. When the input word's size is an odd number, and we have only one letter left on the tape, we can stop to confirm that the word is a palindrome. We will replace and detail the decision step (diamond box) in the above flowchart to bring in this nuance.
3. In the above flowchart, except for the erase operation, we have not specified the specific action between steps. We shall detail that out too. We shall specifically mention the action we would take for the value we encounter in a particular cell on every edge.

Figure 2.3.4 captures a refined version of the earlier flow chart. A detailed description of this technique is articulated right after Figure 2.3.4.

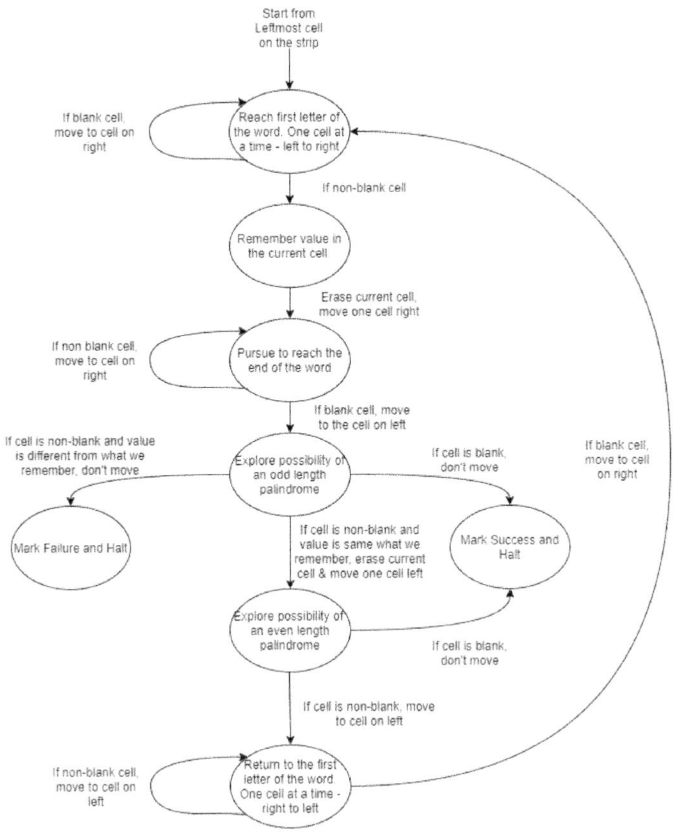

Figure 2.3.4 (Step 2)

Here is a detailed description of the technique.

1. We shall start from the leftmost end of the strip and skip every blank cell on the right until we reach the first letter, i.e., reach the first cell with a 0 or a 1.
2. Once we have reached the first letter, feel and interpret the letter; remember what we have interpreted, erase the cell, and move one cell right in

pursuit of getting to the last letter of the string. We will elaborate on this process in Step 3.

3. If the cell has a nonblank letter, keep moving toward the right to reach the string's last letter. Since we are blindfolded, we shall get to the last letter by skipping every nonblank cell on our way, and once we get to a blank cell, move one step left.
4. Now, we have reached the last cell of the string. If the cell is blank, we can exit with a decision that the string is an odd length palindrome, i.e., a string of length 1, 3, 5, etc. If the present cell has a different letter from what we remember, exit with a decision that the string is not a palindrome. If the cell has a letter that is the same as what we remember, perform the following—erase this letter and move one cell left to see if we have any more letters left as part of our original string.
5. Now that we have entirely erased one pair of letters from either end, we need to see if we have any more letters. In case we have read and interpreted all letters part of the original string, the previous step should have brought us to a blank cell, and in case we are in a blank cell, we can exit with a decision that the string is an even-length palindrome, i.e., a string of length 2, 4, 6, etc. If the cell has a nonblank letter, move one cell left in pursuit of moving toward the left to reach the first letter of the revised string, to repeat the process.
6. Again, as we are blindfolded, we shall reach the first letter of the revised string by skipping every nonblank cell on the left until we get to a blank cell

and then move one step right. Once we are here, we could return to Step 2 and repeat the flow until we exit.

If you find the steps confusing, I urge you to write down a few binary strings on paper (both palindromes and others) and follow through with the above steps to get the hang of the technique. Through the representation in Figure 2.3.4, we have taken a significant step toward formalizing our mental process as a computation method. You might observe that each node in Figure 2.3.4 captures our specific *mental state* (this shall be called state going forward) relevant to a particular step. Each edge captures the specific action we would take when we are at a particular state and encounter a specific letter on the tape. Our thought experiment is technically complete at this moment, but we would need to make one more improvement to the above representation, which would include the following:

- For each node, along with the description of our mental state, we shall give it a code name (S1 through S6). The code names shall be S & F for the Success and failure nodes.
- We shall be more explicit with the letter we deal with at every step. As the alphabet that we have considered has only two letters (excluding a blank), the evolution should be reasonably straightforward. When we do this, you will observe that the "remember" step (Step 2—S2) will get replaced by two parallel paths, one when we encounter a 0 in Step 1 and the other when we encounter a 1.

- We shall give a structure for instructions mentioned at each edge. The structure will have three parts <Present value in the cell, new value in the cell, movement on the tape>. For example, if we encounter a 0 in the current cell in a particular mental state and need to update it to a 1 and move right, we shall represent it as <0, 1, R>. Another example would be that if we encounter a 0 in the current cell in a particular mental state and need to erase it and stay in the same cell, we shall represent it as <0, ƀ, P>. P stands for Stay Put.

Figure 2.3.5 is the transformed version of our earlier flowchart, with the recent refinements incorporated. We have added a few more aspects to our original model with the above representation.

- A set of acceptable states relevant to the solution to the problem.
- Out of these relevant states,
    - We shall mark one state as initial, i.e., the state our computation method begins with at the start of the process. In our thought experiment, this corresponds to our mental state (S1) when we start from the leftmost cell in the strip, searching for the first letter of the string.
    - We shall mark one or more states as final, i.e., the state our computation method arrives at, by the end of the process. In our thought experiment, it is the states S and F.

- A set of rules that define the transition across various states.

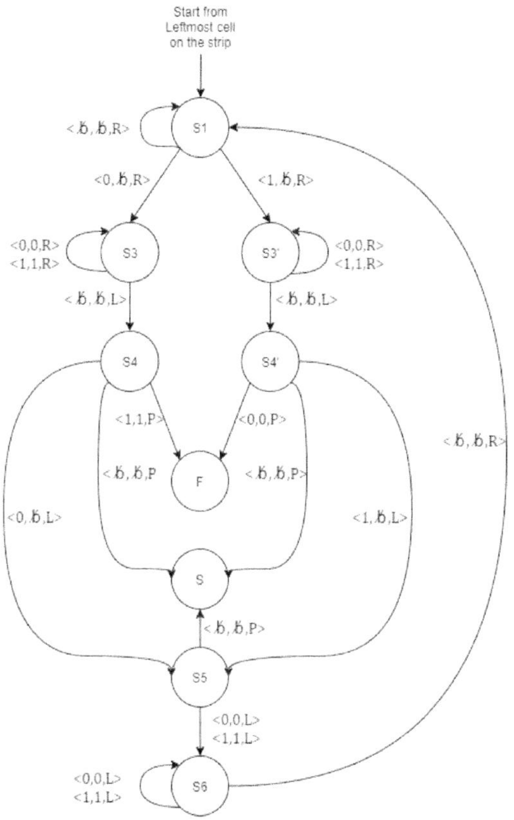

Figure 2.3.5 (Final Step)

For one last time, we shall summarize the various aspects that we have found relevant to the problem at hand.

1. A thin strip of paper where we can print our string.
2. The string can have letters from the binary alphabet, i.e., 0 or 1, and the special symbol ƀ.

3. A set of well-defined operations that would include the following abilities:
    a. To interpret the letter (including a blank) present in a cell.
    b. To move to the next cell (left or right).
    c. To update the value of a specific cell.
4. A set of states that will be relevant as we solve a problem. One would be the initial state, and there can be one or more final states (S & F in our example above).
5. A set of rules that define the transition across various states.

With the above, we have arrived at the complete list of essential aspects to understand the mathematical model that Turing envisioned. Our next chapter will discuss stitching these concepts together and formalizing the model.

2.4 Deterministic Turing Machine

Some of the core aspects that we arrived at in the earlier chapter, especially the tape, are inspired by how we (humans) have conventionally tried to solve computational problems, i.e., over a pen and paper. Before formalizing Turing's theoretical computer model, we must understand one more concept. The concept is *determinism*.

For the palindrome problem, the computation method that we laid out through a flowchart (Figure 2.3.5) in the earlier chapter can also be expressed through a state transition table, captured in Table 2.4.1. The state transition table tries to capture the following: When we are at a specific state and encounter a particular *symbol* (hereon, we shall consider a letter a symbol too) on the tape, what is the precise action we need to take? As discussed earlier, the action will have three parts:

1. The new symbol that we may have to write to the present cell.
2. The direction of the move, i.e., should we move to the next cell on the right, left, or stay put.
3. The next state that we would need to transition to.

Through the flowchart and the transition table, it is pretty clear that, for a specific context, i.e., when we are at one particular state and encounter a particular symbol, we can transition to only one target state. In other words, when we are in a specific state, through the flowchart or the transition table, we can precisely determine that next state upon encountering a particular symbol. When a computation method exhibits this characteristic, the method is deterministic. So, our palindrome solver computation method is deterministic.

State	Symbol on Tape	Write Symbol	Move to	Next State
S1	ƀ	ƀ	R	S1
S1	0	ƀ	R	S3
S1	1	ƀ	R	S3'
S3	ƀ	ƀ	L	S4
S3	0	0	R	S3
S3	1	1	R	S3
S3'	ƀ	ƀ	L	S4'
S3'	0	0	R	S3'
S3'	1	1	R	S3'
S4	ƀ	ƀ	P	S
S4	0	ƀ	L	S5
S4	1	1	P	F
S4'	ƀ	ƀ	P	S
S4'	0	0	P	F

S4'	1	ƀ	L	S5
S5	0	0	L	S6
S5	1	1	L	S6
S5	ƀ	ƀ	P	S
S6	ƀ	ƀ	R	S1
S6	0	0	L	S6
S6	1	1	L	S6

Table 2.4.1

As you notice, with the above transition table, we have made something more evident. What started as a mental process of our palindrome solver has evolved into a transition table with a well-defined set of instructions. A well-defined set of instructions means we now have the possibility of executing these through a machine. Of course, that machine should have the aspects that we discussed earlier. That includes a tape, an ability to interpret symbols, move left and right, and take the instructions laid out in the above table as a configuration. That is the digital computer that Turing envisioned through his theoretical model.

Turing's theoretical model of a computer is an *abstract machine*, defined through a 7-tuple[2] {Q, τ , I, ƀ, q0, F, δ}. Turing's model is an abstract machine because it fundamentally is a

[2] The definition of a DTM through a 7-tuple is from the book The Design and Analysis of Computer Algorithms, authored by Alfred V. Aho, John E. Hopcroft, and Jeffrey D. Ullman.

theoretical model, including physical aspects such as the tape. The specific variation that we shall describe here is single-tape *Deterministic Turing machine*[3] (referred to as a Turing machine or DTM going forward). There is also an m-tape (or multi-tape) version of this machine, which is merely an extension of the single-tape DTM.

1. Q is a set of states.
2. τ is a set of tape symbols.
3. I is the set of input symbols that belong to the alphabet $I \subseteq \tau$.
4. ƀ $\in \tau$ and is in τ - I. ƀ is the special symbol (blank).
5. $q_0 \in Q$ is the initial state.
6. $F \subseteq Q$ is the set of final states.
7. δ is a transition function that maps a subset of (Q -$\{q_f\}$) X τ to Q X τ X {L, R, S} where $q_f \in F$.

Model Spec 2.4.1

Designing an algorithm (or a computation method) for a decision problem that a Turing machine can solve would involve specifying its seven-tuple. For instance, here is the algorithm for our palindrome solver.

1. Q equals {S1, S3, S3', S4, S4', S5, S6, F, S}
2. τ = {0, 1, ƀ}
3. I = {0, 1}

---

[3] In his original paper, Alan Turing named his abstract machine the automatic machine or simply the a-machine, which got named after him later.

4. ƀ is the blank symbol
5. $q_0 = \{S1\}$
6. $F = \{S,F\}$
7. δ is the state transition table expressed in Figure 2.4.1

Model Spec 2.4.2

Here is the schematic representation[4] of the single-tape DTM. With the Read-Write head's help, the Turing machine would interpret and update the symbol in a particular cell.

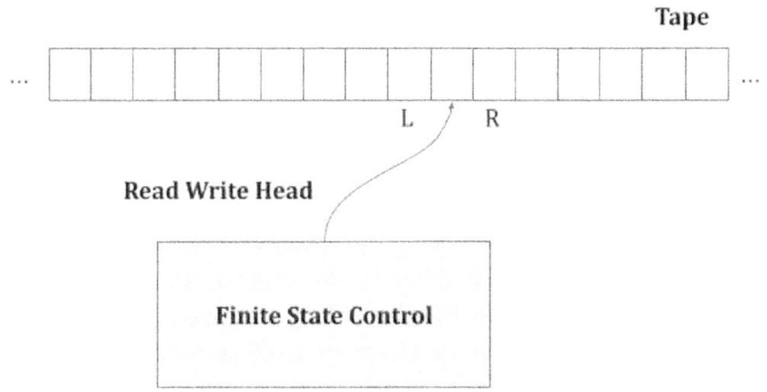

Figure 2.4.1

Through the abstract model (Model Spec 2.4.1 and 2.4.2), Turing precisely articulated what computation meant, something Hilbert had not explicitly defined. Mathematicians and philosophers worldwide generally accepted Turing's abstract machine as they found it reasonable. Through that acceptance, Turing established the working definition of an

---

[4] The schematic representation of the DTM as articulated by Michael R. Garey and David S. Johnson in the book Computers and Intractability.

algorithm, which is nothing but defining the seven-tuple for the Turing machine. In other words, for a specific decision problem, if we can specify its seven-tuple, it means an algorithm exists to solve the decision problem. It is equivalent to the following statement: The decision problem is solvable using a DTM.

Turing further argued that, for a specific decision problem, if we cannot define its solution through the seven-tuple, an algorithm for that decision problem may not exist. Turing went ahead and decisively proved that for some decision problems, algorithms could not exist. Such problems are *undecidable*. He had to identify one decision problem and logically prove that we could not write an algorithm for that problem. What is that crucial problem? The one that Turing chose was the Halting problem[5]. We will get to see that in detail in the subsequent chapters, but before that, we need to build more intuition, which we shall begin doing right away.

[5] In the Appendix section, we shall discuss the Halting problem and Turing's proof of why it is undecidable.

3. DEFINING THE PROBLEM SPACE

3.1 Why Decision Problems?

Now that we have defined the theoretical model (of a computer) in the form of a Turing Machine, our subsequent pursuit will be about finding its limits. We have seen that the Turing machine is a simple construct that can solve various problems. But how do we find its actual limits? One way would be to attempt and devise algorithms to solve all possible problems, which may not be feasible. The other possibility could be to choose a problem set representing the overall problem space smartly. This chapter is about identifying that *representative problem set* that we shall use to measure the limits of the Turing machine in the subsequent chapters.

In one of our earlier chapters, we defined decision problems. To recap, decision problems are a class of problems that can be posed as a Yes/No (or true/false) question. Decision problems were a natural choice for Turing as he challenged the decidability aspect of Hilbert's program. There are certain other advantages of choosing Decision Problems as our representative set. Before we discuss those, let us look at some of the other popular classes of problems—*Optimization Problems* & *Search Problems.*

Optimization Problems are a class of problems that involve identifying an optimal solution. A classic example is the *Traveling salesman problem* (TSP) that goes by the following description: Given a set of cities and distances between each pair of cities, what is the shortest path one can take by visiting each city once and returning to the origin city?

Another interesting optimization problem is the *knapsack problem* that goes by the following description: Given a set of items, each with a specific weight and a value, how could we identify the things that can go into the knapsack such that we meet the following two conditions:

- The overall weight of the knapsack does not exceed a limit.
- The overall value of the knapsack, i.e., the cumulative sum of the items' values, is maximized.

You could think of a knapsack as a regular backpack.

Search Problems are another class of problems that involve identifying a structure x in another object y. For example, in a textbook with n chapters, what chapters have the word *computation*? In this example, the word computation is the structure x, and all words across all chapters are object y.

All of the problems mentioned above, be it TSP, the knapsack problem, or the search problem, are different from decision problems. We cannot answer these with a simple yes or no. In the case of the TSP, the solution is a collection of cities that would signify the visits' sequence. In the case of Knapsack, the solution is a list of items and their quantity, and in the case of the search problem, the solution is a list of chapter names.

Though search and optimization problems are equally popular, there is an advantage to decision problems. We can *recast* both search, and optimization problems as a decision problem, and here is how we could transform the three problems (TSP, Knapsack, and search a word) that we described above.

1. Is there a loop that goes through all the cities whose total distance is at most x miles?
2. Is there a combination of items that we can identify that have a value of at least v?
3. Does the word computation occur in at least n chapters?

It might be evident through the above examples that we can recast a search or an optimization problem by applying either a lower bound or an upper bound. In other words, the decision variant is about solving a specific instance of the original problem. For example, while TSP is about finding the shortest path, the decision variant is about validating whether a path of a particular length exists. But wait, then we are not solving the same problem, correct? That observation is accurate, but we will solve the optimization problem through the decision variant with a few additional steps. Here is how we could do that to solve the TSP.

To recap, here is the decision variant of TSP—Is there a loop that goes through all the cities whose total distance is at the most x miles? Let us assume we already have an algorithm for this decision problem, and we'll call it A. This algorithm will take a list of cities, the distance between pairs of cities, and the input value x as input. In other words, we shall initialize the Turing machine with these values on the tape and the seven-tuple specification corresponding to algorithm A. If the Turing machine can find a path of length less than x then it would halt with the Success state, leaving the last explored path (with a total distance less than x) on the tape. If the Turing machine cannot find any path whose total distance is less than x miles, it would halt in the Failure state. The tape will be empty in this state, i.e., all cells will be blank.

Using the above algorithm for the decision problem, we can solve the original problem, i.e., finding the shortest path through the following steps. The seven-tuple specification corresponding to these steps shall become an algorithm to solve the Optimization problem using another Turing machine.

- Step 1: Identify any loop that touches all cities, calculate the total distance (say d) of that loop, and assign it to x. This loop may or may not be the shortest path.
- Step 2: Let us assume the identified loop is not the shortest path and reassign x to $d/2$, i.e., the midpoint between 0 and d.
- Step 3: Run through the steps of algorithm A with the revised value of x. If we get a Success this time, we may have a loop with a shorter path to our original loop, i.e., between 0 and $d/2$. If not, we can infer that the shortest path is between $d/2$ and d.

- Step 4: If the previous step was a success, reassign x to a new midpoint, i.e., $d/4$. If the last step was a Failure, assign x to $3 * d/4$ and go to Step 3.

Algorithm 3.1.1

As we follow the above steps, we will converge and arrive at the shortest path in a finite set of steps, to be precise, in $log(d)$ iterations. We have illustrated the solution path in Figure 3.1.1.

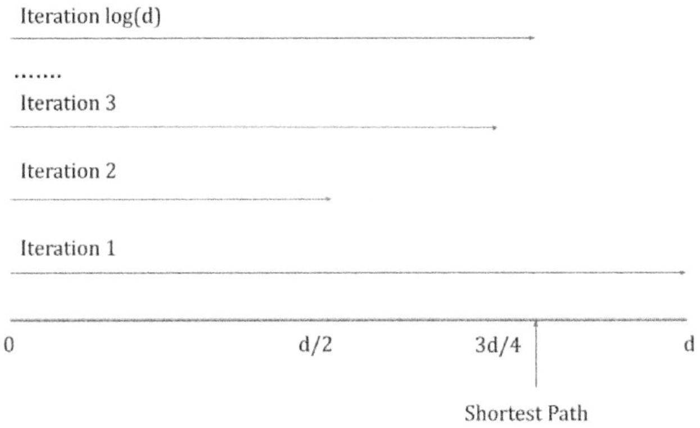

Figure 3.1.1

The above technique involves splitting the solution space by half until we converge on the solution. This technique is a popular one that goes by the name *binary search*. We could apply a strategy similar to Algorithm 3.1.1 to solve the original versions of Knapsack and search problems through their decision variants. This ease of transformation is another crucial reason why Decision problems can be an appropriate representative problem set to test the Turing machine's limits.

In our journey to understand the $P\ vs. NP\ Problem$, our focus shall only be on decision problems. Now that we have carved out our problem space to consist of all decision problems (Figure 3.1.2), we shall identify different classes of problems within this space in the subsequent chapters. This classification will be based on the algorithm's characteristics to solve those decision problems. In other words, we shall begin filling the below canvas (Decision Problems canvas) step by step.

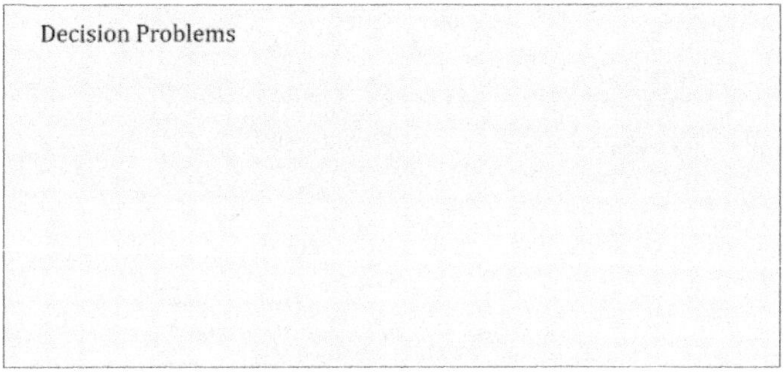

Figure 3.1.2

With the above transformation of problems, you might have noticed that, though we could solve the original optimization and search problems through their decision variants, we could do that only by introducing additional steps. If we introduce other steps, are we compromising on the solution's efficiency? That's an important question, and to answer that, we would need to define an algorithm's efficiency. In our next chapter, we shall define that and use that to compare different algorithms and, more importantly, test the Turing machine's limits.

3.2 Measuring Efficiency

So far, we have defined the theoretical model (of a computer) and have a working definition of an algorithm. We also need a way to measure and quantify the *efficiency of an algorithm.*

Efficiency is determined based on how complex an algorithm is, and the complexity of an algorithm reflects the number of resources it requires to solve a problem. The resource is generally the time to completion. Still, because the Turing machine is a theoretical model of a computer, we shall consider one state transition to be one unit of time. If an algorithm takes fewer state transitions to reach the Success state than another, we will regard that as relatively efficient or less complex.

To understand complexity, we shall derive our Palindrome solver algorithm's complexity by quantifying the number of state transitions required to solve an input string of length n. We have provided the state transition flowchart on the following page that we had arrived at in our earlier chapters. Also, the exact state transition paths are captured in the following table (Table 3.2.1) for a few scenarios.

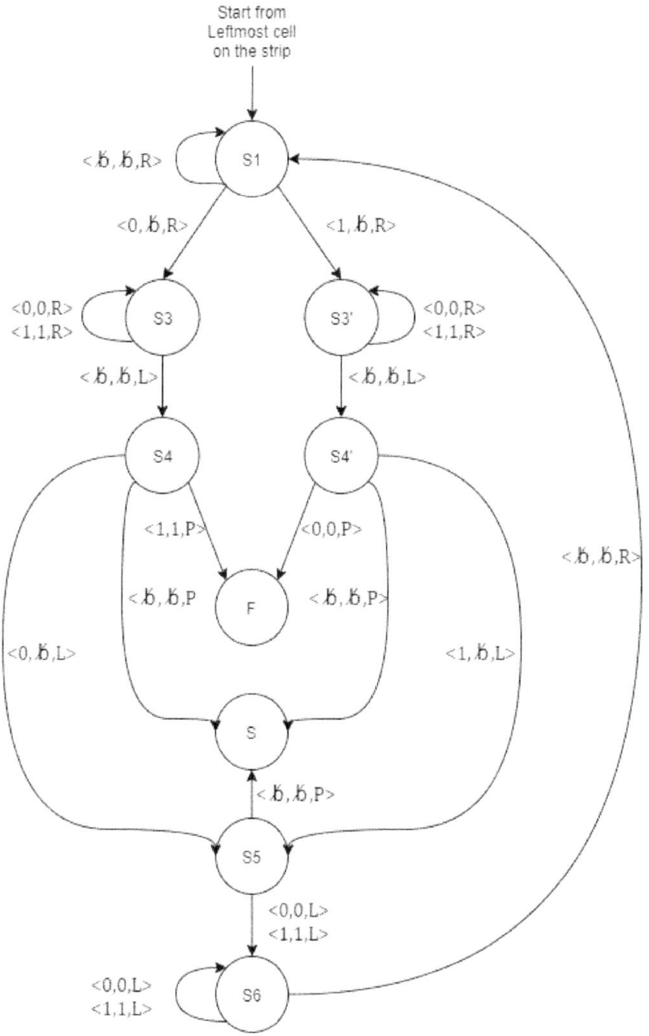

Figure 3.2.1

As you might observe in table 3.2.1, we shall not consider the initial state transitions (between S1 and S1) until we reach the first nonblank symbol in the tape. Also, if a state transition path for a string involves a substring whose transition path is already derived, we shall not break down the path of the substring. For instance, as $S(1111)$ involves $S(11)$, the expression for $S(1111)$ will directly refer to $S(11)$.

Input String (i)	**State Transition** $S(i)$	**Length of Input String (n)**	**State transition path before reaching "Success" state**	**Number of state transitions before "Success" state** $S(n)$
0	$S(0)$	1	S1-S3-S4-S	3
11	$S(11)$	2	S1-S3'-S3'-S4'-S5-S	5
101	$S(101)$	3	S1-S3'-S3'-S3'-S4'-S5-S6- $S(0)$	10
1111	$S(1111)$	4	S1-S3'-S3'-S3'-S3'-S4'-S5-S6-S6- $S(11)$	14
11011	$S(11011)$	5	S1-S3'-S3'-S3'-S3'-S3'-S4'-S5-S6-S6-S6- $S(101)$	21
111111	$S(111111)$	6	S1-S3'-S3'-S3'-S3'-S3'-S3'-S4'-S5-S6-S6-S6-S6- $S(1111)$	27

Table 3.2.1

In the table above, you might observe that we have only considered successful scenarios, and there is a reason for the same. For two input strings of identical length, where one is a palindrome, and the other is not, the number of state transitions is always higher for the palindrome string. From that standpoint, a successful scenario captures the worst-case scenario for the Palindrome solver. Also, while the state transitions could vary for different input strings, the number of transitions before reaching the success state would be the same for two different input strings of the same length. For instance, the state transitions would be ten for the following input strings—111, 000, 010, and 101. Next, we shall dissect the transition path into five phases. We shall split the transition path into the following:

1. State transition(s) to reach the rightmost blank cell from left: We shall refer to the count of state transitions in this phase as S(L-R).
2. State transition(s) to turn back and switch directions: In our transition table, this corresponds to the following state transitions S3-S4 or S3'-S4' (Direction shift 1). We shall refer to the count of state transitions in this phase as S(DS1).
3. State transition(s) to reach the leftmost blank cell from right: We shall refer to the count of state transitions in this phase as S(R-L).
4. State transition(s) as we move to the Success state or the next loop: In our transition table, this corresponds to the following state transitions: S4-S or S5-S, or S6-S1 (Direction shift 2). We shall refer to the count of state transitions in this phase as S(DS2).

5. State transition(s) to solve the remaining string whose length is two less than the original length (n): We shall refer to the count of state transitions in this phase as S(n-2).

In the below table (Table 3.2.2), we have provided a dissected version (by five phases) of the previous table (Table 3.2.1).

Input String (i)	**State Transition** $S(i)$	**Length of Input String (n)**	**State transition path before reaching "Success" state**	**Number of state transitions before "Success" state** $S(n)$
0	$S(0)$	1	S1-S3-S4-S	3 [1+1+0+1+0]
11	$S(11)$	2	S1-S3'-S3'-S4'-S5-S	5 [2+1+1+1+0]
101	$S(101)$	3	S1-S3'-S3'-S3'-S4'-S5-S6- $S(0)$	10 [3+1+2+1+3]
1111	$S(1111)$	4	S1-S3'-S3'-S3'-S3'-S4'-S5-S6-S6- $S(11)$	14 [4+1+3+1+5]
11011	$S(11011)$	5	S1-S3'-S3'-S3'-S3'-S3'-S4'-S5-S6-S6-S6- $S(101)$	21 [5+1+4+1+10]
111111	$S(111111)$	6	S1-S3'-S3'-S3'-S3'-S3'-S3'-S4'-S5-S6-S6-S6-S6- $S(1111)$	27 [6+1+5+1+14]

Table 3.2.2

A summarized version of the above table focusing only on the transition count is provided below.

Count of State Transitions by Phase	Length of the input string (n)					
	1	2	3	4	5	6
S(L-R)	1	2	3	4	5	6
S(DS1)	1	1	1	1	1	1
S(R-L)	0	1	2	3	4	5
S(DS2)	1	1	1	1	1	1
S(n-2)	0	0	3	5	10	14
Total - $S(n)$	**3**	**5**	**10**	**14**	**21**	**27**

Table 3.2.3

Let us now try to generalize the number of state transitions, i.e., express $S(n)$ as a function of the length of the input string n.

$$S(n) = S(L-R) + S(DS1) + S(R-L) + S(DS2) + S(n-2)$$

$$S(n) = n + 1 + (n-1) + 1 + [(n-2) + 1 + (n-3) + 1 + S(n-4)]$$

$$S(n) = n + (n-1) + (n-2) + (n-3) + 4 + S(n-4)$$

$$S(n) = n + (n-1) + (n-2) + (n-3) + .. + 1 + n + 1 \text{ when n is odd}$$

$$S(n) = n + (n-1) + (n-2) + (n-3) + .. + 1 + n \text{ when n is even}$$

$$S(n) = \frac{n^2}{2} + \frac{3n}{2} + \mathbf{1} \text{ when n is odd}$$

$$S(n) = \frac{n^2}{2} + \frac{3n}{2} \text{ when n is even}$$

Through the above set of equations, we have quantified the complexity of our palindrome solver. But do we have to remember the two polynomial equations? Isn't there a more straightforward representation of our algorithm's complexity?

Yes, there is an abstraction, and before we understand that, we need to observe how our complexity function $S(n)$ grows relative to n^2. Why n^2 ? The reason is, our complexity equation is a second-degree polynomial, and n^2 has a higher growth rate compared to n. If our complexity equation happens to be a third-degree polynomial, our choice should be n^3.The below table captures the growth rate of our complexity functions $S(n)$ and n^2.

n	$S(n)$	n^2
1	3	1
2	5	4
3	10	9
4	14	16
5	21	25
6	27	36
7	36	49
8	44	64
9	55	81

Table 3.2.4

As you might observe, leaving the initial three values of n (1, 2, and 3), $S(n)'s\ value$ remains less than n^2. More importantly, the gap widens between $S(n)$ and n^2 as n grows. Our complexity function $S(n)$ is *asymptotically bounded* (will also be referred to as *upper-bounded* or *bounded* going forward) by n^2. An equivalent way of saying this is $S(n)$ is on the order of n^2. A more conventional way to say the same thing in Computer Science would be—$S(n)$ is $O(n^2)$. This notation (O) is called the *Big-O notation*, and we shall be using this notation from hereon to measure and compare the efficiencies of different algorithms.

From the previous paragraph and the table provided in Table 3.2.4, it must be clear that n^2 by itself is a good approximation and abstraction of the complexity of our palindrome solver algorithm. This way, we don't have to remember the two polynomial functions that we derived for $S(n)$. We could conclude that our palindrome solver's complexity is $O(n^2)$, or the algorithm is on the order of n^2. Here is a quick practice—Algorithms that are $O(n^2)$ are more efficient (or less complex) than $O(n^3)$ algorithms. Algorithms that are $O(n)$ are more efficient (or less complex) than $O(n^2)$ algorithms.

3.3 P class of Problems

In the previous chapter, we quantified our Palindrome solver algorithm's complexity and concluded that it was $O(n^2)$. We are aware that the expression n^2 is a second-degree polynomial. We can make our original statement differently—the palindrome solver algorithm can solve the decision problem in *polynomial-time*. We shall classify decision problems of this kind as $P\ class$ of problems where P stands for polynomial-time. Yes, we have succeeded in formally defining our first class of decision problems with this.

All algorithms that are $O(n^2)$ belong to the $P\ class$ of problems. To be precise, any algorithm whose complexity equation is a *k-degree* polynomial belongs to the $P\ class$ of problems. In other words, this class includes all problems whose solution complexity is $O(n^k)$ where $k \geq 0$. Also, the complexity equation of specific algorithms is not polynomial but *logarithmic* (of base 2). For instance, the complexity of the binary search technique that we briefly elaborated on in one of the previous chapters (Figure 3.1.1) is $O(log(n))$. Some of the *sorting methods* (*quicksort* and *merge sort*) have a worst-case complexity $O(nlog(n))$. Though these algorithms' complexity is nonpolynomial, i.e., logarithmic, since polynomials like $n\ and\ n^2$ bound logarithmic functions like $log(n)\ and\ nlog(n)$, these problems shall also be considered part of the $P\ class$ of problems. We can see this relation in the following table, where we compare the growth rates of logarithmic and polynomial functions. We can see $log(n)$ is bounded by n , and $nlog(n)$ is bounded by n^2 .

n	$log(n)$	$nlog(n)$	n^2
1	0	0	1
2	1	2	4
3	1.58	4.75	9
4	2	8	16
5	2.32	11.61	25
6	2.58	15.51	36
...	...	...	...

Table 3.3.1

I hope you have got the hang of state transitions in a Turing machine now. From here on, for easy reading, when we discuss algorithms, we shall not use state transition tables but a pseudo-code of a high-level programming language (Python styled).

Switching to pseudo-code would not change the complexity, which would remain the same as the algorithm's seven-tuple specification that we would use to solve using a DTM.

Let us practice this through a simplified version of a python-style algorithm written to *bubble sort* (ascending order) an array of n integers.

```
arr = [11, 10, 32, 2, 31,50,99,9]
# input_length variable will hold the length
# i.e. 8
input_length = length(arr)
# Traverse through all subarrays starting with
# the largest and push the largest value to the end
for i_loop in range(input_length-1, 0, -1):
        for j_loop in range(0,i_loop):
        # For each pair of values, push the
        # larger value to the right
                if arr[j_loop] > arr[j_loop+1] :
                        temp=arr[j_loop]
                        arr[j_loop] = arr[j_loop+1]
                        arr[j_loop+1] = temp
                end
        end
end
```

Algorithm 3.3.1

As you might observe above, the essence of bubble sort is the following:

1. The outer loop (i_loop) starts with the entire array and pursues pushing the largest number to the array's last slot. The largest number is pushed by comparing pairs of values through the inner loop (j_loop).
2. Once the largest value is pushed to the last slot, repeat the above step for the array, excluding the last slot (aka subarray), attempting to move the second-largest value to the penultimate slot.
3. Repeating the above two steps seven times, i.e., one less than the previously considered subarray would

get all the values in their respective positions of a sorted array.

How shall we measure the complexity of the above algorithm? Similar to the number of state transitions in a DTM, the count of comparisons (Line 9 in Algorithm 3.3.1) required for an array of size n is an appropriate estimate of the algorithm growth. The comparison step is inside two *for* loops, and if we attempt to count the total comparisons required for an array of size n, we arrive at the following complexity function:

$$S(n) = (n-1) + (n-2) + \ldots.3 + 2 + 1$$

$$S(n) = n(n-1)/2$$

$$S(n) = \frac{n^2}{2} - \frac{n}{2}$$

As you might observe, the complexity of bubble sort is $O(n^2)$ and falls under the P *class* of problems.

You might wonder what the significance of this classification is and that will become clearer as we identify the next important class of problems. We shall first understand certain aspects that make some problems hard to solve.

Before that, we shall conclude by adding the P *class* of problems to our canvas.

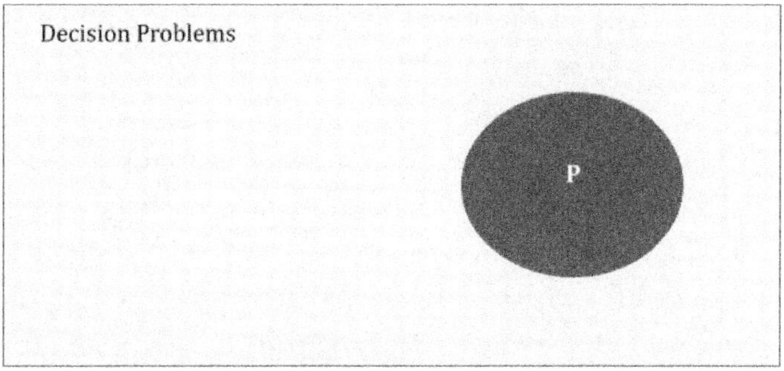

Figure 3.3.1

3.4 Hard Problems

When I was a kid, my mom told this story many years ago. Long ago in India, there lived a king who was very bored with his humdrum life. He challenged his team of ministers to invent something interesting for him, maybe a new game that did not exist. One of his sharp ministers, who also happened to be his advisor, came back with an innovative board game that two players can play on a sixty-four square board, with each player having sixteen pieces (at the start of the game). Each piece had a unique power, and the board game setup mimicked a real-life battlefield. That marked the birth of the game of modern-day *chess*.

The king loved the game so much that he wanted to reward the minister for his invention. He asked the minister what it was that he would like to have. The minister was modest and stated that the thought of wanting to reward is itself a big reward. But the king was so happy that he insisted the minister ask something. Upon the king's insistence, the minister thought for a while and responded that he had something in mind, but the king may not offer that. The king was offended. He asked, *How can there be something that I'll not give you? State what you need.* The minister responded with a smile. *I would like to receive a certain quantity of rice.*

Hearing that, the king was both baffled and relieved. *Rice? that we have in plenty. How many tonnes do you need?* Responded the king. The minister replied *I would like you to calculate that.*

As the game I invented had sixty-four squares, start with placing one rice grain in square one. Now, double that and place those many grains in the next square, i.e., place two grains on square 2 and continue this for the entire sixty-four squares (place four grains in square 3, eight grains in square 4, and so on). Whatever number you arrive at in square 64, give me as many grains.

Phew! Is that all that you need? Consider it done. The king immediately ordered one of his deputies to arrange that at the earliest. A few days later, the deputy arrived with a panic-struck face. Upon inquiry, the deputy stated, *We started to calculate the number of grains for the reward, and by the time we reach half of the board, we foresee that we would have exhausted the entire supply of rice that we can produce this year. The number is growing faster than we had imagined.* The legend is that the king realized his mistake and apologized to the minister for his miscalculation. The king also promised to be more watchful before making any promises in the future. Having accomplished what he intended to do, the minister let go of his fake wish and remained an advisor for the king for years to come.

That's the power of exponential equations. For incremental values of n, *exponential functions*, i.e., 2^n grow much faster than the other two functions, i.e., logarithmic and polynomial. Not only with rice, but exponential growth can also quickly exhaust any of the finite resources that we would have at our disposal. The number of state transitions that an algorithm takes to solve certain decision problems would also suffer from this exhaustion. Here is a quick comparison of the growth rate of the three functions.

n	$log(n)$	$nlog(n)$	n^2	2^n
1	0	0	1	1
2	1	2	4	4
3	1.58	4.75	9	8
4	2	8	16	16
5	2.32	11.61	25	32
6	2.58	15.51	36	64
7	2.81	19.65	49	128
8	3	24	64	256
...	...	...	...	...

Table 3.4.1

Like the chess challenge, solutions to some problems may look deceptively simple but practically *intractable* because the best algorithm for these problems takes at least $O(2^n)$ time. Here are some specific intractable problems.

- TSP
- Subset sum problem
- Knapsack problem

Apart from intractable problems, two other kinds of decision problems are hard to solve. The first kind of problems are those that are undecidable. The difference between intractable and undecidable problems is that, for undecidable problems, we cannot (leave alone efficiency) even have an algorithm to solve them. Yes, it is not that we don't have a solution, but we can also prove that a solution is impossible using a Turing Machine. The Halting Problem is an example of an undecidable problem.

The other kind of problems are those that we have tried to solve in vain and remain unsolved. For these problems, we neither have an intractable solution nor have proven that they are undecidable. An example is the Kth Largest subset sum problem.

To summarize, we have identified three kinds of decision problems that are hard, and that includes problems that are:

- Undecidable
- Intractable (and)
- Unsolved

We shall go through each of the above problems in detail, and we will begin exploring the TSP in the subsequent chapters.

But before that, let us include this classification of hard problems in our Decision Problem canvas.

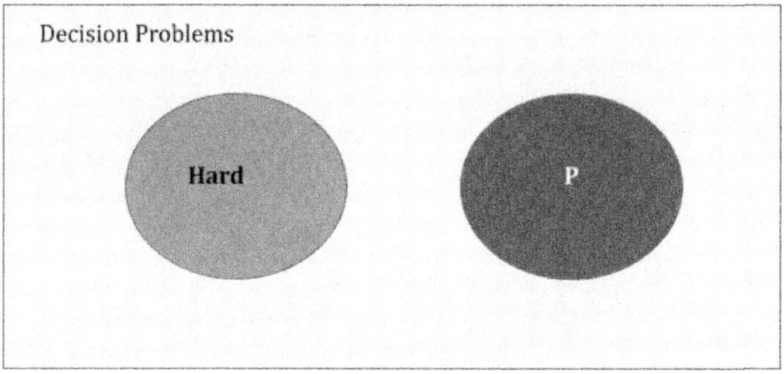

Figure 3.4.1

4. LEAP OF FAITH

4.1 Nondeterminism

Through the chapters in this section, we will lay the foundation of one of the most critical concepts in theoretical Computer Science. Grasping this idea is key to our journey in understanding the *P vs. NP Problem*. The idea is *Nondeterminism*, and it is also arguably one of the most misunderstood concepts among students and practitioners. Nondeterminism can be confusing for many, and there can be a few reasons for that. The first reason is its abstractness, i.e., we do not have an actual implementation of nondeterminism in any form yet. Second and more importantly, understanding this concept in its entirety would involve a *leap of faith.* I call it a leap of faith because nondeterminism will require us to believe that sometime in the future, we will find efficient solutions to problems that are intractable today. This section will build all the necessary intuition and motivation that necessitated the birth of nondeterminism.

In the earlier chapter, we discussed three kinds of hard problems: *undecidable, unsolved, and intractable.* Intractable problems are those for which we do not have efficient or polynomial-time solutions using a DTM. The best solutions we have for many of these take $O(2^n)$ time. While we cannot do much about undecidable hard problems and those we have tried to solve in vain, i.e., unsolved, what about intractable problems? Though algorithms were possible using a DTM, they were of little use owing to their inefficiency. To computer scientists and mathematicians, this was frustrating.

The general pursuit among computer scientists and mathematicians back then was to find a way to transform an algorithm with exponential complexity into an algorithm with polynomial complexity. For instance, even if the transformation step takes an overhead through an $O(n^{100})$ algorithm, it is still a big win, as n^{100} would grow slower than 2^n for larger values of n. Despite these efforts, it was evident that efficient solutions to specific problems will remain unknown. Well, at least for the near term. In a way, history has supported that, i.e., these algorithms remain intractable even after the evolution of sophisticated processors in the past several decades. Foreseeing that, mathematicians' focus shifted toward devising a framework to capture that *unknown* and eventually learn to manage that unknown.

In this section of chapters, we shall understand the unknown and build the intuition for a framework to capture the unknown. In the next section, we will take this framework further to manage the unknown. Let us understand the specific aspects of these hard problems that make their solutions intractable. We shall do that through a short thought experiment. Some of you might be familiar with the hedge maze from *The Shining* movie. For a moment, imagine ourselves at the entrance of that maze. Remember, we have not had an aerial view of that labyrinth. Given that, what would be our strategy at every crossroad? If we were the child shown in the below figure[6], what path would we take?

Figure 4.1.1

For now, we shall only consider mazes that are free of loops. With no prior knowledge about the maze, there are a few different strategies that we could adopt, like the wall follower technique, Tremaux's algorithm, and others. None of these techniques are efficient because they will let us explore some needless paths when we adopt this in the real world. The important limitation that we are bound to face with every algorithm is that, at every crossroad, we *cannot determine* or *choose* what is the right path until we take that path. It is precisely this aspect that makes some algorithms intractable, and this is the unknown that we are talking about.

[6] The source of the image is Pixabay.com

Let us see if we realize the above limitation in another hard problem. The problem we shall consider is the decision version of TSP, which goes by the following description: Given a set of cities and distances between each pair of cities, is there a loop that goes through all the cities whose total distance is at the most d miles? We will work out the complexity of the TSP through an example. In our example, we will consider four cities (named A, B, C, and D), and one can reach each city from every other city in more than one way. Figure 4.1.2 shows a graph that depicts the various paths across the four cities and the distance between every pair of cities.

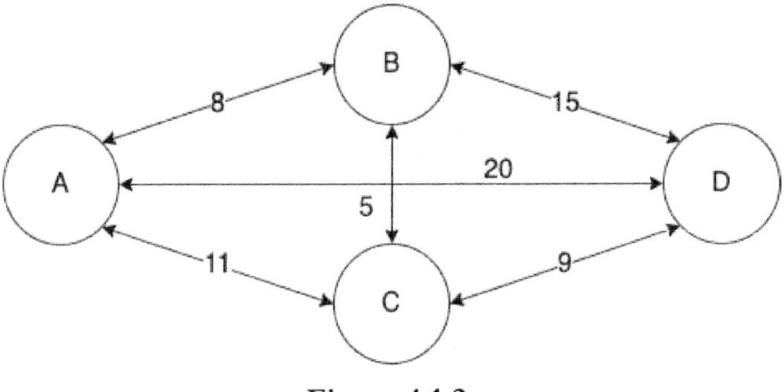

Figure 4.1.2

The crux of the algorithm we will consider is articulated in Algorithm 4.1.1. The algorithm considers two sets —X and Y and a utility function Distance(X).

- X: An ordered set of cities
- Y: Set of cities
- Distance (X): To calculate the total distance as we move from one city to another in a specific sequence

and return to the first city. For instance, when X = {A,B,D,C} then Distance(X) = 43 (8+15+9+11).

There are three steps to the algorithm:

1. Initialization step: Initialize the starting city and the input distance d.
2. Calculation step: Calculate the shortest path by calling the Shortest_Path function.
3. Verification step: Remember, we are solving a decision problem, so the algorithm would need to respond with a Yes or No. To provide that response, we would need to verify, i.e., compare the calculated value with the input value.

The steps of the algorithm are annotated in python style (#).

```
# Initialization step
# Initialize the problem and the starting state
d=<input distance>
X={A}
Y={B,C,D}

# Calculation step
# Calculate the shortest loop starting from a specific city. In
#  this case, the city is A

Shortest_loop=Shortest_Path(X,Y)

# Verification step
# To return a Yes or No based on how the shortest
#  loop compares against the input distance.
If Shortest_loop <= d
        Return Yes
```

```
Else
        Return No

# The below function to be called to calculate the shortest
# loop from a specific city that touches all the cities in Y
Shortest_Path (X, Y)
{
        If Y is empty:
                Return Distance(X)
        Else:
                minimum_distance=<some high value>
                For each city c in Y:
                        Remove c from Y
                        Append c to X
                        # Recursively calculate the
                        # minimum distance
                        Minimum_distance =
                                min(minimum_distance,
                                Shortest_Path (X,Y))
                        Remove c from X
                        Add c to Y
        return(minimum_distance)
}
```

Algorithm 4.1.1

As you might observe through the above algorithm, the shortest path from a particular city is calculated through the Shortest_Path function *recursively*. The concept of recursion is for a program to call itself with a different value. This function simulates the possible traversal paths across the four cities through the for loop and recursion. If we were to plot the algorithm's path (Shortest_Path function) through a state tree (or) solution tree, here is the pictorial representation of the same.

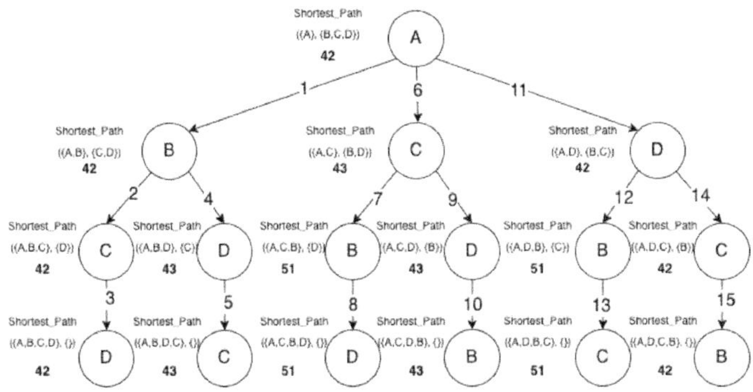

Figure 4.1.3

There are a couple of points to be noted from the above state tree.

1. We can see the actual call made to the Shortest_Path function at every node. We can also see the value that will eventually be calculated and stored in the variable minimum_distance.
2. At every edge, there is a number that depicts the sequence of the call. As you might observe, leaving the initial call to the Shortest_Path, there can be at most fifteen recursive calls to the Shortest_Path function before determining the shortest path from city A.

How do we calculate the algorithm's complexity, i.e., Shortest_Path function? Similar to how we figured the complexity of bubble sort in Chapter 3.3, we could count the number of times the comparison is made, i.e., the number of times the mininum_distance value is calculated (underlined statement in Algorithm 4.1.1). This count corresponds to the number of nodes in the state tree depicted in Figure 4.1.3. For four cities, the number of comparisons is sixteen, and for five cities, the number of states in the state tree will be sixty-four. The complexity to calculate the shortest path from one specific city is $n!$

$$S(n) = n!$$

So, how does $n!$ (factorial) grow? The below table would give us a sense of the growth rate of $n!$ and how it compares with the other functions. Factorial grows much faster than the exponential counterpart.

n	$log(n)$	$nlog(n)$	n^2	2^n	$n!$
1	0	0	1	1	1
2	1	2	4	4	2
3	1.58	4.75	9	8	6
4	2	8	16	16	24
5	2.32	11.61	25	32	120
6	2.58	15.51	36	64	720
7	2.81	19.65	49	128	5040
8	3	24	64	256	40320

Table 4.1.1

Wait, did we not say that the complexity of TSP is exponential? Yes, that is correct. The above algorithm uses a primitive method (*backtracking*) to arrive at the optimal path. However, in 1962, Mathematicians Bellman, along with Held and Karp, independently arrived at a slightly more efficient algorithm (called Bellman–Held–Karp algorithm) to solve TSP, and that is $O(n^2 2^n)$. Though $O(n^2 2^n)$ algorithm is more efficient than $n!$ algorithm, both are intractable on a DTM for large values of n.

As we observe the state tree for TSP, its similarity with our maze problem may be evident. The intractability arises from our inability to choose the next city. Just the way we were unable to choose the right path at a crossroad of the maze, here too, we are unable to find our next city to visit until we explore all paths across every city. It's not only with TSP or the maze problem, but this inability exists for many problems we have classified as hard and whose solutions are intractable using a DTM. The intractability arises because we cannot make the right choice without trying out all possible traversal paths. In the knapsack problem, our inability would be in choosing the next item. Similarly, in the subset problem, our inability would be in selecting the next appropriate number from the collection, and so on.

We will believe that we will acquire that ability (to make the right choice) in the future. Until then, we will assume that a black box would supplement that capability. The black box is a *Guesser*, i.e., a guessing module that can help us make the right choice in polynomial-time. To be precise, our guesser can efficiently make the right choice in $O(1)$ time.

We shall invoke the guessing module to make the right turn at a crossroad (in the maze) or choose the next city to visit when solving TSP.

In essence, the Guessing module can help determine what we cannot decide now, which forms the crux of nondeterminism.

We shall invoke the Guessing module by invoking the *guess* operation, and the algorithms we would write leveraging this module are *nondeterministic algorithms.* Here is the nondeterministic version of a solution to TSP.

```
# Initialization step
# Initialize the problem and the starting state
d=<input distance>
X={A}
Y={B,C,D}
n=length(Y)

# Calculation step
# Calculate the shortest loop starting from a specific city. In
# this case, the city is A
For i=1 to n
        # Find the next city to visit through the guessing
        # module
        next_city=guess(X,Y)
        Append next_city to X
        Remove next_city from Y
Shortest_loop = Distance(X)

# Verification step
# To return a Yes or No based on how the shortest loop
# compares against the input distance.
```

```
If Shortest_loop <= d
        Return Yes
Else
        Return No
```

Algorithm 4.1.2

As you might observe, the algorithm involves guessing the next city to visit from set Y through the guess operation. What would be the complexity of the nondeterministic algorithm's calculation step mentioned in Algorithm 4.1.2? We know that the guess operation's complexity is assumed to be $O(1)$, and the module is executed $(n-1)$ times. Therefore,

$$S(n) = n - 1$$

Hence, $S(n)$ is $O(n)$, i.e., polynomial. In essence, through nondeterminism, we have arrived at an algorithm that can solve TSP in polynomial-time.

Now, you might wonder what would have motivated the smartest minds to formalize the concept of nondeterminism and believe in the possibility of a guesser, i.e., a guessing module. First and foremost, most of what we know today, we did not know earlier. In the example of TSP, our original algorithm had a complexity on the order of $n!$ However, we learned a better algorithm through Bellman, Harp, and Held. In a way, we refuse to believe (until proven otherwise) that, just because we are unable to arrive at an efficient algorithm today, we will remain like this forever. Second, until we find a solution, we need an effective way to package what we don't know today to progress on the other theoretical aspects related to computing. The concept of nondeterminism addressed both, and we shall deliberate this a bit more in the following chapters.

Though we have introduced the guesser capable of doing what we cannot do, i.e., making the right choice in $O(1)$ time, can we use it to guess anything? Not really, and there is a method to it. If you observe in the above examples, we have used the guesser to make the right choice out of a finite set of choices. In the case of TSP, the choices are the various cities, and in the case of the maze problem, the choices were the paths available at every fork. The choices should be finite and manageable to deploy a guesser in our algorithm. In other words, we should generate the set of choices in polynomial-time.

Before we move forward, there is one last thing we would need to keep in mind. Remember, we have only guessed the shortest path with the guesser's help through the calculation step. But the original problem is to solve the decision version of the optimization problem for TSP. That would require one additional step to verify if our guess was correct. After we complete guessing, i.e., after we complete the calculation step (in both the algorithms shared in Figures 4.1.3 and 4.1.6), there needs to be a *verification* step to determine if the guessed shortest path is indeed less than the input distance d. If you notice, unlike the calculation step, the verification step is relatively straightforward, i.e., it does not require the help of a guessing module.

In other words, the verification can be solved using a DTM in polynomial-time. Analogous to a Rubik's Cube, where it is a trivial task to verify if a cube is solved compared to solving the cube itself, not just TSP, for many decision problems that are hard to solve, it is straightforward to verify its solution. We will know more about this in the next chapter.

4.2 Nondeterministic Turing Machine

Our pursuit of understanding the world through numbers has not been free of surprises. Once in a while, during their research, mathematicians stumble upon tricky situations in the form of unforeseen and challenging problems. Some of the issues were so hard that it appeared there was no way out from them. Time and again, mathematicians have found ingenious ways to overcome those obstacles and make progress. Here, I would like to cover two such instances from history. We will also see how mathematicians tackled them to keep the research moving.

The first is when mathematicians encountered the square root (principal square root) of -1, i.e., $\sqrt{-1}$. The notion of numbers is likely to have come to existence when our forefathers felt the need to group and count real objects such as animals or members of the tribe. Natural numbers (1, 2, 3, etc.) are the most primitive in a set that includes all numbers. Through multiple discoveries, motivated either through complexities of life or curiosity, mathematicians pursued and discovered numbers that are nontrivial and that included negative numbers (numbers such as −1, −2), fractions (rational numbers such as $\frac{1}{2}$), and irrational numbers ($\sqrt{2}$, π). Yet, stumbling upon something like $\sqrt{-1}$ was unsettling for mathematicians as it appeared unsolvable. Leonhard Euler, a Swiss mathematician, overcame this challenge by introducing the i*maginary number* i ($i^2 = -1$), giving birth to a whole new branch in algebra called complex numbers.

The second instance is when mathematicians encountered an infinite series during their research. Here is an example.

$$A = 1 - 1 + 1 - 1 + 1 - 1 + 1 - 1 \ldots\ldots \infty$$

Infinite series was another curveball thrown at mathematicians, who struggled because they could not quantify an endless series like the one shown above. That was not until Srinivas Ramanujam, a mathematician from India, ingeniously solved the puzzle the following way:

$$A = 1 - 1 + 1 - 1 + 1 - 1 + 1 - 1 \ldots\ldots \infty$$
$$1 - A = 1 - (1 - 1 + 1 - 1 + 1 - 1 + 1 - 1 \ldots\ldots \infty)$$
$$1 - A = 1 - 1 + 1 - 1 + 1 - 1 + 1 - 1 \ldots\ldots \infty$$
$$1 - A = A$$
$$2A = 1$$
$$A = \tfrac{1}{2}$$

Intractable problems are another curveball thrown at us, and through the concept of nondeterminism, we shall overcome the DTM's limitation. At the beginning of the earlier chapter, we had stated that our pursuit in this section would be to arrive at a framework that will help us capture the unknown. Extending the concept of nondeterminism, we shall precisely arrive at that framework by the end of this chapter.

In the previous chapter, we had written a nondeterministic algorithm for TSP. Earlier, we had also defined an algorithm as a computation method that can be solved using a Turing machine. But we know, we cannot simulate a nondeterministic algorithm, i.e., an algorithm that involves a guessing module using the DTM. To write nondeterministic algorithms, we would need to conceptualize a Turing Machine variant that can interpret nondeterministic algorithms. The variant is the *Nondeterministic Turing Machine* (NTM).

Before we get into the details of the NTM, let us attempt to plot the state tree or solution tree of the nondeterministic algorithm for TSP that we designed in the previous chapter.

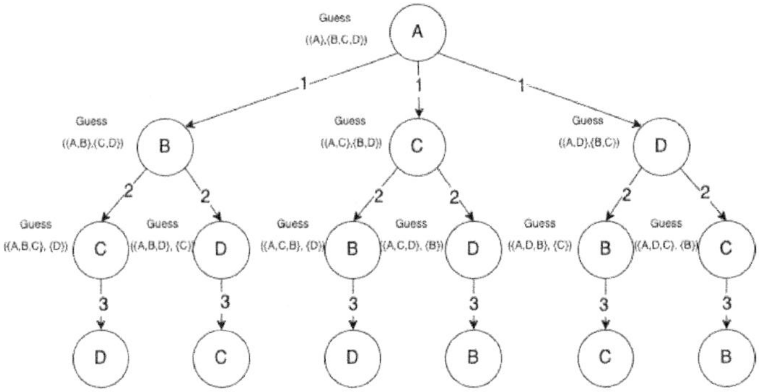

Figure 4.2.1

The similarities of the above solution tree with its Deterministic variant (Figure 4.1.3) might be evident to you. However, there are two crucial differences that we would need to understand.

1. The first difference between the algorithm variants of DTM and NTM lies in the sequence step that you see on every edge. In the Deterministic variant of the TSP algorithm, the sequence step is unique, i.e., we have to go through a specific path before we explore the other. However, in the nondeterministic algorithm, the guess operation is $O(1)$, so the solution is attainable in three steps, i.e., $n-1$ steps for n cities. An NTM can accept a configuration with more than one target state for the same input value, which is the defining characteristic of an NTM.
2. In the NTM variant, we are not solving for the shortest distance at every node but merely guessing our next move. After making the required guesses, we would need to validate through a verification step if we have guessed the solution. We would have seen this in the earlier chapter as we devised the algorithm for solving TSP. This verification process must be possible in polynomial-time.

Like the DTM, we shall define an NTM through a seven-tuple {Q, τ , I, ƀ, q_0, F, δ}. The only difference is how we prescribe the transition between states through δ. As mentioned above, in an NTM, there can be more than one target state prescribed for a specific combination of state and input symbol on the tape. In essence, δ is a *transition relation* for an NTM, whereas it is a *transition function* for a DTM.

I urge you to compare and contrast the seventh point in Model specification 4.2.1 with the DTM (Model spec 2.4.1).

We should be careful about the interpretation of an NTM. Though NTM allows transitions to more than one state, it does not mean parallel execution, and missing this point is common among students. The correct interpretation of the sequence step (in Figure 4.2.1) is—while there are multiple paths from each state, the guesser component would help us take the right step in $O(1)$ time.

1. Q is a set of states.
2. τ is a set of tape symbols.
3. I is the set of input symbols that belong to the alphabet $I \subseteq \tau$.
4. ƀ $\in \tau$ and is in $\tau - I$, which is the special symbol (blank).
5. $q_0 \in Q$ is the initial state.
6. $F \subseteq Q$ is the set of final states.
7. δ is a transition relation $(Q - \{q_f\}) \times \tau \times (Q \times \tau \times \{L, R, S\})$ $q_f \in Q$.

Model Spec 4.2.1

Putting all these together, here is the schematic representation[7] of the one-tape NTM. We can visualize an NTM as a DTM augmented with a guessing module. The guessing module shall help us make the right choice at every step in $O(1)$ time. The guess shall be written back to the tape

[7] The schematic representation of the NTM as articulated by Michael R. Garey and David S. Johnson in the book Computers and Intractability.

by the guesser, which the NTM will pick up for further processing.

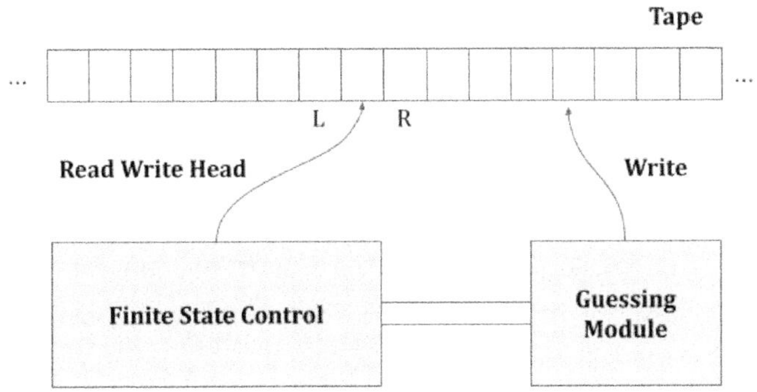

Figure 4.2.2

4.3 NP class of Problems

Let us summarize what we have learned so far in this section. We started this section with the concept of nondeterminism by going through the various motivations that led to its birth.

We then detailed the construct of an NTM and went through the anatomy of a nondeterministic algorithm. Essentially, an NTM would solve an intractable problem in polynomial-time (taking the guesser's help) whose solution would take exponential time when solved using a DTM. Whether identifying the next city to visit (in TSP) or choosing the direction to take (in the maze), we saw how an NTM could help package what we wouldn't know while solving hard problems. The intuition behind NTM is not to realize its physical implementation but to perform thought experiments in our pursuit to arrive at solving hard problems.

We defined the NTM as a seven tuple and showed how it differs from a DTM. The critical difference between the DTM and the NTM lies in how the state transitions are defined. In DTM, the transition between states is a function, i.e., there can be no more than one target state from the current state upon encountering a specific symbol on tape. In the case of an NTM, the transition is a relation, i.e., there can be more than one target state configured from the current state upon encountering a specific symbol on tape.

At the beginning of this section, we articulated that our pursuit would be to arrive at a framework to capture what remains unknown. This chapter will use all the concepts we have learned to formalize that framework. The framework is the *NP class* of problems. Through this classification, we shall group decision problems for which we do not have efficient solutions, i.e., decision problems that are intractable, using a DTM. So, what is the *NP class* of problems? *NP* stands for Nondeterministic Polynomial, and it includes decision problems that have the following characteristics:

1. We can design nondeterministic algorithms and solve the problem using an NTM in polynomial-time; and
2. We can verify their solutions in polynomial-time using a DTM.

The second characteristic is as essential as the first (primary) characteristic. Many hard problems will exhibit these characteristics. Even when a decision problem does not show these, in most cases, we would be able to transform them (similar to the way we transformed the optimization variant of TSP) into decision problems that would exhibit the above characteristics. Informally, we can phrase the ***P vs. NP problem*** the following way: *every problem whose solution can be quickly verified can also be solved quickly?* The reasoning for this is the second bullet point mentioned above.

We are now ready to plot the *NP class* of problems in our canvas. What decision problems could we consider part of *NP class*?

We went through TSP and touched upon Knapsack and Subset Sum problems, which meet the above criteria. So, we know that the *NP class* includes some hard problems. What about the decision problems part of *P class*? Problems in *P class* can be solved in polynomial-time using a DTM. We reviewed that the only difference between NTM and DTM is the transition relation. While DTM can have only one target state, NTM can have more than one target state. From that standpoint, DTM is only a special case of an NTM. Therefore all *P class* problems will naturally become part of *NP class* of problems.

What about problems that lie outside of *P class* and Hard problems? Remember, we haven't identified the boundaries of *NP class* of problems yet. We haven't proved that *NP class* exists only within *P class* or the class of problems we had classified as hard problems. Therefore, we will have to assume that *NP class* will spread outside the *P class* of problems and Hard problems unless we can prove otherwise.

Given the above understanding, let us go ahead and add the *NP class* of problems to our Decision Problem canvas.

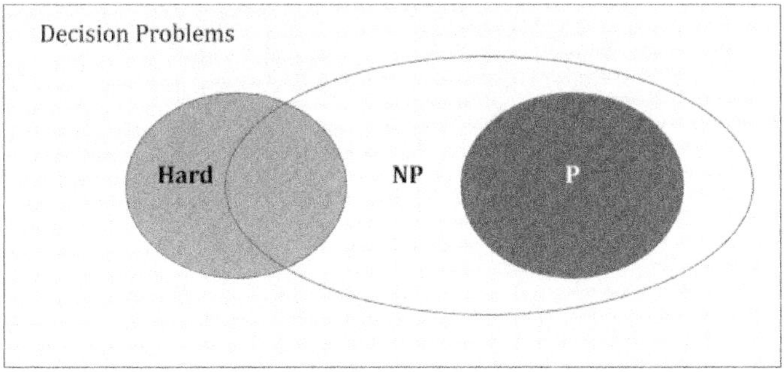

Figure 4.3.1

5. MANAGING THE UNKNOWN - PART 1

5.1 The Master Problem

Is there anything similar between *Product Advertising* and the *Arms Race*? What looks different on the surface could fundamentally be the same underneath. When competing companies that offer identical products spend money on advertising, they try to get the consumers' mindshare in the market away from the competition. But remember, money spent on an advertisement would eventually need to be borne by the consumers only by paying more for the same product. Increased prices might also work against the company. Given this scenario, to maximize their payoffs (revenue, new customers), it might sound optimal for companies to reduce their spending on advertising. But that hardly happens. Why is that? The rationale might be apparent through the below payoff matrix. The numbers in each cell are the first company's payoffs and the second company for their specific choices.

Company A \ Company B	Don't Advertise	Advertise
Don't Advertise	200,200	0,400
Advertise	400,0	50,50

Figure 5.1.1

As you might observe, though the individual payoffs are high (two hundred points each), if both choose not to advertise, there is no incentive to adhere to it as a company can suffer if competition decides to advertise. Hence, both will promote and realize a suboptimal payoff (fifty points each).

Let us now see the scene between two countries engaged in a cold war. Both the countries would desire to have a military advantage over the other. In that pursuit, both would pump more and more money to remain a superpower. Here again, the result is a suboptimal state as articulated through the following payoff matrix:

Country A \ Country B	Don't build Nuclear Weapons	Build Nuclear Weapons
Don't build Nuclear Weapons	300,300	100,400
Build Nuclear Weapons	400,100	200,200

Figure 5.1.2

As mentioned earlier, the numbers in the matrix above quantify the party's payoff (increased revenue in the first scenario and acquired military advantage in the second scenario), which are likely to be determined by different mathematical models. Yet, the conflict's essence made evident through the structure of the payoff matrix is the same. They are similar because these problems are manifestations of the *Prisoner's Dilemma* in *Game Theory*. So, what is the prisoner's dilemma, and how is it similar to the above scenarios?

Consider a scenario where two partners (A and B) commit a crime. They get arrested by the cops and are imprisoned and kept in individual cells with no way to communicate with each other. Unfortunately, the prosecutors lack enough evidence to press on the principal charge, and they only have enough evidence to convict both of them for a lesser charge. Given this, the cops offer a bargain to both A and B independently. Each of them is offered to be set free but on one condition. The condition is that they would need to defect, i.e., betray the other partner by testifying that the other partner committed the crime. The other option each partner has is to cooperate and remain silent. Remember, partners A and B cannot communicate with the other. So both are unaware of what the other person is thinking. Figure 5.1.3 shows the payoff matrix for the Prisoner's dilemma.

Partner A \ Partner B	Co-operate	Defect
Co-operate	-1,-1	-3,0
Defect	0,-3	-2,-2

Figure 5.1.3

Advertising, Arms race, and Prisoner's dilemma deal with the fundamental conflict in game theory. Conflict is the clash between individual and group interests. In summary, if we had solved the Prisoner's dilemma, we would have solved the other two. Unless we resolve the clash between individual and group interests, all three will remain unsolvable.

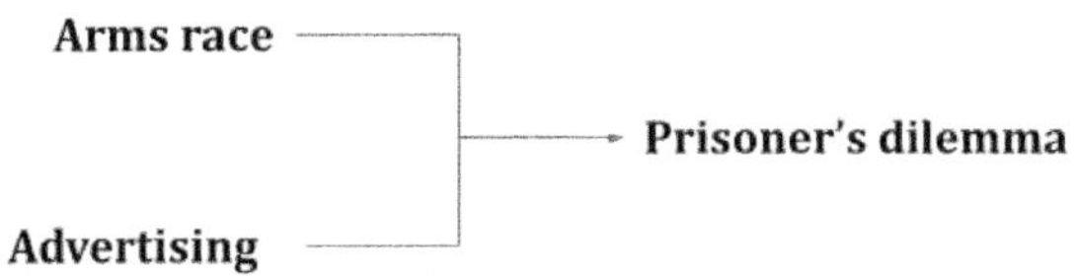

Figure 5.1.4

You might wonder what relevance the prisoner's dilemma holds in $P\ vs.NP\ Problem$. When it became evident to mathematicians and philosophers that hard, intractable problems are here to stay, their pursuit of finding efficient solutions slowly shifted toward finding ways to manage the unknown. The search then gravitated toward identifying commonalities between these intractable problems to arrive at one fundamental problem or at least fewer problems that we could transform all intractable problems into. That way, we could spend our effort solving that fundamental problem and not all. The catch here is, if the transformation was to be possible, it ought to happen in polynomial-time through a DTM, and there is no point if this transformation itself is intractable or if it requires an NTM. Technically, the transformation between two problems in polynomial-time (using a DTM) is called *reduction.* When we transform problem A to problem B in polynomial-time using a DTM, we reduce problem A to problem B. Reducing A to B is expressed as $A \alpha B$. Reduction also implies, we can design a solver for A using the solver for B, which we have conceptually depicted in the below figure.

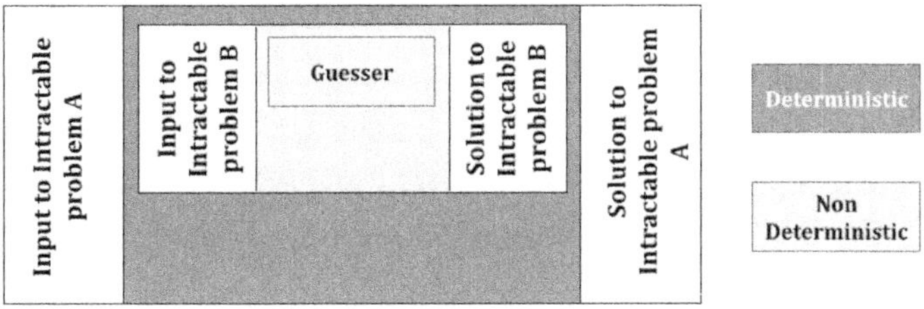

Figure 5.1.5

The pursuit was essentially to identify something similar to the Prisoner's dilemma among these intractable problems classified under *NP class*. Can we transform these intractable decision problems into fewer problems or one *master problem*? Suppose we can arrive at that master problem. In that case, we can design solvers for all problems that belong to *NP class* using a solver that solves that master problem. Figure 5.1.6 captures this idea.

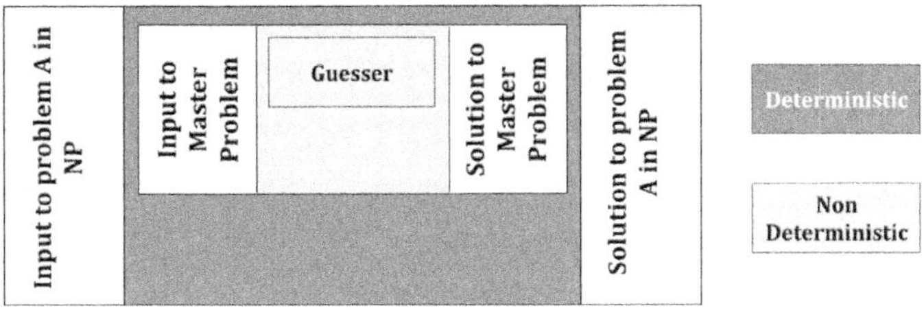

Figure 5.1.6

Before we understand this, let us explore if commonality exists between decision problems. We shall do that by exploring another intractable problem—*The N Queens problem.*

The N Queens problem is a scenario where we have an $N \times N$ chessboard, and the challenge is about placing N Queen pieces on the board such that none of the queens attack each other. Here is the solution to the problem on a 4×4 chessboard, i.e., when $N = 4$. In this chessboard, the rows are numbered 1 through 4, and the columns are numbers A through D.

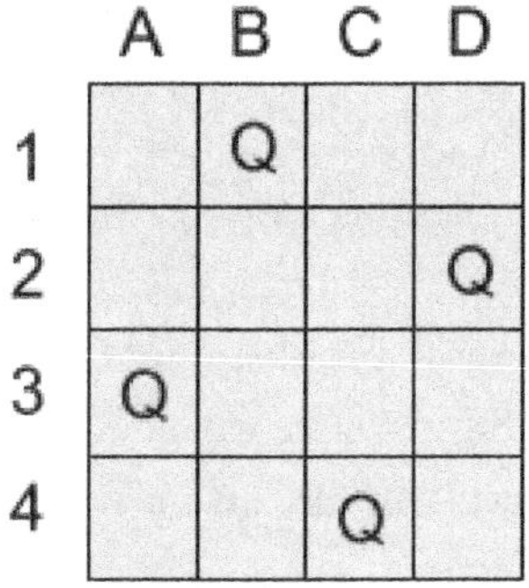

Figure 5.1.7

Figure 5.1.8 shows the partial solution tree for the N Queens decision problem where $N = 4$. The solution tree starts with the initial state I, and for every row, the right choice is made through the guesser module to determine the Queen's placement on that particular row. The number of levels in the tree corresponds to the number of rows on the chessboard. The path led by the highlighted nodes in the below figure corresponds to the solution path. We will determine the solution after making four calls to the guesser module (or N calls for an $N \times N$ board).

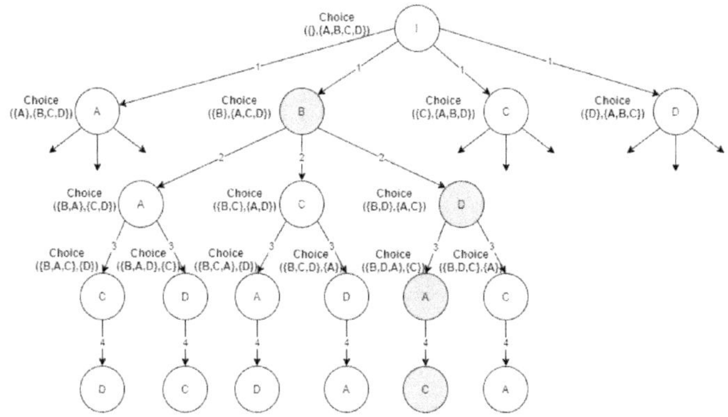

Figure 5.1.8

If you observe, except for node I and the edges that come out, the subtree starting from the second row is the same tree that we had arrived at to solve TSP using an NTM. Figure 5.1.8 has one additional level because we had one of the cities as a starting point in TSP. So, there is evidence of commonality among intractable problems. But, does a fundamental problem exist to transform all of these intractable problems into one? Yes, such a fundamental problem does exist, and it is the *Boolean Satisfiability problem*, also called the *SAT problem* in short form. We shall delve into the details of it in the next chapter.

5.2 Boolean Satisfiability Problem

Around the late sixties and the early seventies of the twentieth century, while the mathematicians' community was still trying to tackle these intractable problems, a new concept emerged, which later got christened $NP - completeness$. One of the pioneers of this concept was Stephen Cook, an American Canadian mathematician, who made an important discovery in 1971 through his paper titled *The Complexity of Theorem-Proving Procedures.* Around the same time, another Soveith American mathematician Leonid Levin had made the same discovery through his independent research.

The findings of Stephen Cook and Leonid Levin, now known as the *Cook–Levin Theorem*, were a significant breakthrough in Computer Science. So, what does the Cook–Levin theorem state, and what was the discovery? The discovery was a unique problem in the $NP\ class$ called the Boolean Satisfiability (SAT) problem to which all problems in the $NP\ class$ could be reduced to, as expressed in Figure 5.2.1.

This discovery is the essence of Cook–Levin's theorem that stated the SAT problem as an $NP - complete$ problem. What do we mean by $NP - complete$? Before that, let us understand the SAT problem in detail.

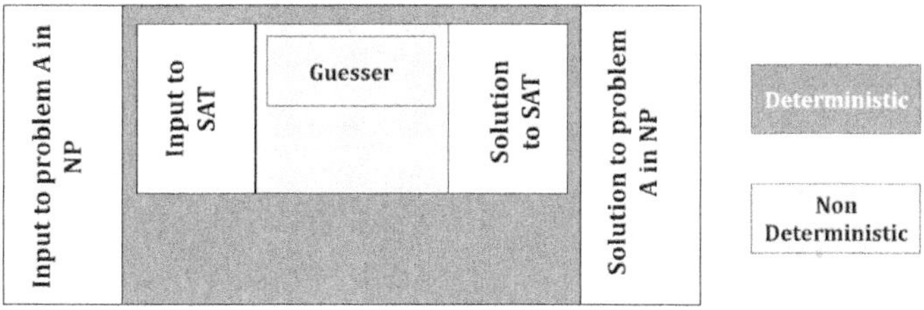

Figure 5.2.1

Boolean Satisfiability problem or propositional satisfiability problem (will be referred to as SAT going forward) is the problem of determining if there exists an assignment of input values for which the given Boolean expression is satisfied, i.e., is there a combination of input values for which the expression returns true? For instance, out of the following two Boolean expressions, the first is satisfiable when $x_1 = x_2 = 1$. However, the second expression is not satisfiable for any assignment of x_1. In essence, statement (1) is satisfiable, and statement (2) is unsatisfiable. The symbol $\vee$ corresponds to Boolean OR operation, symbol $\wedge$ corresponds to Boolean AND operation, and symbol $\neg$ corresponds to the NOT operation.

$$(x_1 \vee x_2) \qquad (1)$$

$$(x_1 \wedge \neg x_1) \qquad (2)$$

The specialty is that we could reduce all problems in *NP class* (including the intractable ones) to SAT in polynomial-time. We have provided Mathematical proof for the same as part of the appendix. But in this chapter, we shall see the transformation of a problem to SAT through an example, and the problem that we shall take is *Sudoku.*

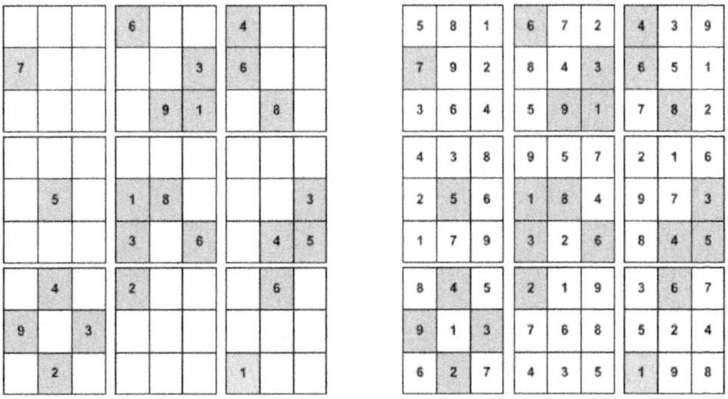

Figure 5.2.2

As you might be aware, Sudoku is a popular math problem found in newspapers across the globe. The above figure shows that the problem involves filling missing cells of a 9×9 grid with nine subgrids. The following rules shall govern what fills each cell in the grid.

1. We need to fill every empty cell in the grid with a number between 1 and 9.
2. Each cell in the grid can have only one value.
3. A number in a cell cannot repeat in the same row.
4. A number in a cell cannot repeat in the same column.
5. A number in a cell cannot repeat with the same subgrid.

To keep it simple, we shall go through a smaller version of sudoku, i.e., a 4 × 4 grid with four subgrids. We will articulate a scalable solution for 9 × 9 grids and beyond. For the 4 × 4 version, all the above rules remain the same except rule number 1. A number in a cell can be between 1 and 4. A sample 4 × 4 problem is provided below.

1	2		
		2	
	1		2
2			4

Figure 5.2.3

The below figure shows the solution tree of the above 4 × 4 grid on an NTM that will provide a solution in nine steps, i.e., after making nine choices for each blank cell. The grid with numbers in bold shows the solution path.

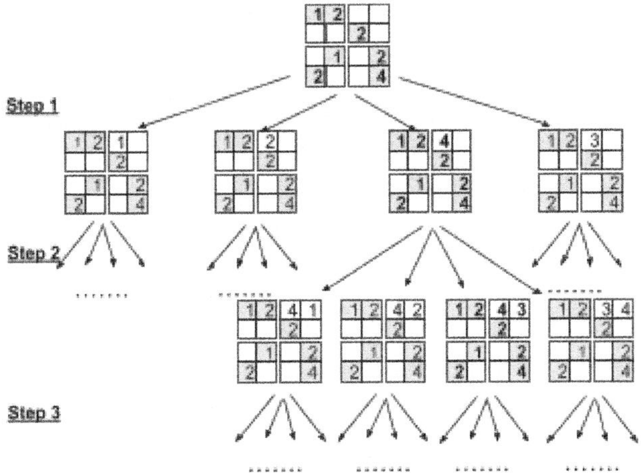

Figure 5.2.4

How do we transform the above problem into a SAT problem, i.e., a Boolean expression of the kind shown earlier? We shall perform the transformation through the following encoding steps:

1. For a 4 × 4 sudoku grid, starting from top left, we shall number and refer to each of the sixteen cells from <1,1> through <4,4>.
2. We shall introduce four Boolean variables for each cell and call it x_{ijk}. This variable's value will be 1 if cell $<i,j>$ has a value of k and 0 otherwise. Variables $i,j,$ *and* k can hold any value between 1 and 4. For the above example, here is the assignment to the Boolean variables corresponding to the cell <1,1>.

$$x_{111} = 1$$
$$x_{112} = 0$$
$$x_{113} = 0$$
$$x_{114} = 0$$

3. We will start building the Boolean expression by applying the earlier five governing rules. Using Rule #1 would mean performing an AND($\wedge$) operation across the expression $x_{ij1} \vee x_{ij2} \vee x_{ij3} \vee x_{ij4}$ for each cell $<i,j>$. In essence, the Boolean expression for Rule #1 (R1) would be:

$$(x_{111} \vee x_{112} \vee x_{113} \vee x_{114})$$
$$\wedge$$
$$(x_{121} \vee x_{122} \vee x_{123} \vee x_{124})$$
$$\wedge$$

$$(x_{131} \vee x_{123} \vee x_{113} \vee x_{114})$$

....

$$(x_{441} \vee x_{442} \vee x_{443} \vee x_{444})$$

4. Rule #2 might look redundant but is required. This rule essentially means that if a cell has a specific value, the same cell cannot have any other value, i.e., if a cell has 1, the cell cannot have 2, 3, or 4. In Propositional logic, conditional statements like these, i.e., *if A is true then B is true* (or *if A is true then B is false*), are expressed as $A \Rightarrow$B. The catch here is that this statement is True, even when A is False. Logically, $A \Rightarrow$B is equivalent to $\neg(A \wedge \neg B)$. Applying conditional reasoning to Rule #2, we would arrive at the following expression (R2):

$$x_{ij1} \Rightarrow \neg(x_{ij2} \vee x_{ij3} \vee x_{ij4})$$

$$\wedge$$

$$x_{ij2} \Rightarrow \neg(x_{ij1} \vee x_{ij3} \vee x_{ij4})$$

$$\wedge$$

$$x_{ij3} \Rightarrow \neg(x_{ij1} \vee x_{ij2} \vee x_{ij4})$$

$$\wedge$$

$$x_{ij4} \Rightarrow \neg(x_{ij1} \vee x_{ij2} \vee x_{ij3})$$

5. Encoding of Rules 3, 4, and 5 will be similar. The encoding for Rule #3 (R3) restricts multiple occurrences of the same number in the same row. The below encoding is only for the first column in the grid, and the complete encoding would involve expanding this to the remaining three columns.

$$x_{i11} \Rightarrow \neg(x_{i21} \vee x_{i31} \vee x_{i41})$$
$$\wedge$$
$$x_{i12} \Rightarrow \neg(x_{i22} \vee x_{i32} \vee x_{i42})$$
$$\wedge$$
$$x_{i13} \Rightarrow \neg(x_{i23} \vee x_{i33} \vee x_{i43})$$
$$\wedge$$
$$x_{i14} \Rightarrow \neg(x_{i24} \vee x_{i34} \vee x_{i44})$$

6. Encoding of Rule #4 is similar to Rule 3 and is provided below (R4). The below encoding is only for the first row in the grid, and the complete encoding would involve expanding this to the remaining three rows.

$$x_{1j1} \Rightarrow \neg(x_{2j1} \vee x_{3j1} \vee x_{4j1})$$
$$\wedge$$
$$x_{1j2} \Rightarrow \neg(x_{2j2} \vee x_{3j2} \vee x_{4j2})$$
$$\wedge$$
$$x_{1j3} \Rightarrow \neg(x_{2j3} \vee x_{3j3} \vee x_{4j3})$$
$$\wedge$$
$$x_{1j4} \Rightarrow \neg(x_{2j4} \vee x_{3j4} \vee x_{4j4})$$

7. Encoding of Rule #5 is slightly different from the other two. For every cell $< i,j >$, no other cell in the same subgrid $< i',j' > \neq < i,j >$ should have the same value. Here is the expression for Rule #5 (R5):

$$x_{ij1} \Rightarrow \neg(x_{i'j'1})$$

$$\wedge$$

$$x_{ij2} \Rightarrow \neg (x_{i'j'2})$$

$$\wedge$$

$$x_{ij3} \Rightarrow \neg (x_{i'j'3})$$

$$\wedge$$

$$x_{ij4} \Rightarrow \neg (x_{i'j'j4})$$

The complete encoding for our Sudoku problem would be an AND of the five independent expressions R1 through R5, i.e., $R1 \wedge R2 \wedge R3 \wedge R4 \wedge R5$ for all values of $i \, and \, j$.

Thus, the Sudoku problem's solution is reduced to determining the above Boolean expression's satisfiability, i.e., finding the specific assignments (0 or 1) for variables x_{ijk} such that the above expression is true. Since we can reduce all problems in $NP \, class$ to a Boolean expression, SAT got a special status among its peers as it captured the essence of the $NP \, class$ completely. SAT isn't any other problem in $NP class$ but also an $NP - complete$ problem.

5.3 NP-Completeness

In the previous chapter, we built the intuition of SAT and its specialty of being the first $NP - complete$ problem. Why is the discovery of the SAT problem considered an important breakthrough in Computer Science? One primary reason is that, like the Prisoner's Dilemma, SAT helped identify an underlying pattern among the many intractable problems. There are more reasons for its specialty that we shall unravel. But before that, let us understand some interesting properties of reduction in general.

Consider three problems from $NP\ class$: P, P', $and\ P''$. If we know that $P \alpha P'\ and\ P' \alpha P''$, i.e., problem P reduces to P' and problem P' reduces to P'', what can we learn from $P\ and\ P''$? It is intuitive that $P \alpha P''$, i.e., problem P reduces to P'', and this is the transitive property of reducibility. What can we learn if we know that problem P reduces to P', and that problem P is $NP - complete$? As problem P is $NP - complete$, we understand that we can reduce all problems in $NP\ class$ to problem P. Also, given that P reduces to P', through the transitive property, we can deduce that all problems in $NP\ class$ can also be reduced to P', which means problem P' is also $NP - complete$.

The above deduction is crucial as this opens up the possibility that $NP - complete$ is indeed a class of problems that can grow beyond SAT. To include problem P

(that is part of $NP\ class$) to the $NP - complete$ class, all we need to do is to reduce a known $NP - complete$ problem to problem *P*. Karp exploited this in 1972 who used Cook–Levin's theorem to identify various other problems that other intractable problems could be reduced to.

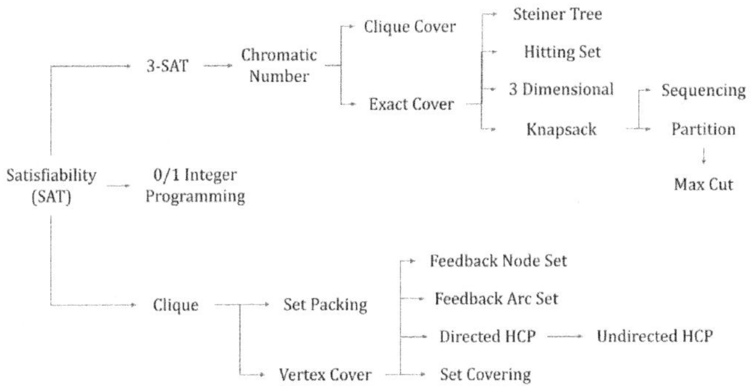

Figure 5.3.1

The above figure captures twenty problems that SAT can be reduced to, either directly or indirectly, through another problem. Karp took Satisfiability as the base problem and reduced it to another problem in the $NP\ class$, i.e., he worked out an algorithm that completes in polynomial-time using a DTM to arrive at other intractable problems. That way, he was able to show that there were many other problems beyond SAT that are also $NP - complete$. Did Karp complicate our pursuit through this activity? We just arrived at SAT to be an $NP - complete$ problem, and solving that single problem would help us solve all problems in $NP\ class$, right? Now, have we introduced more problems to solve? Not really. Karp has improved the possibility of finding tractable solutions to intractable problems if you think about it. By reducing SAT to twenty other problems, Karp has enhanced the count of $NP-complete$ problems to twenty-one from one. Remember, many mathematicians and philosophers were solving different hard problems at that time. Some were thinking about TSP, some about Knapsack, some about Subset Sum, etc. Not all of them had to solve the SAT problem; they only needed to solve the problem they were already researching. Even if one of them succeeded, we would have a tractable solution to all $NP\ class$ problems because all $NP\ class$ problems can be reduced in polynomial-time to another $NP-complete$ problem through SAT.

Karp was instrumental in establishing the methodology of $NP-completeness$. That methodology helped and continues to help structure the research and analysis of hard computational problems that we continue to discover every day. For his contributions, Karp won the Turing Award in the year 1985. Karp's discovery of these $NP-complete$ problems motivated many mathematicians and computer scientists worldwide, who went ahead and discovered hundreds of $NP-complete$ problems since then. When we encounter a new decision problem that we suspect is hard, it would be wise to check if it is an $NP-complete$ problem before spending our time and energy solving it. A decision problem is $NP-complete$ if our answer to the following two questions is *yes*.

1. Does the Decision Problem belong to the $NP\ class$ of problems? i.e., is the problem verifiable using a DTM (in polynomial-time) and solvable using an NTM (in polynomial-time)?
2. Can SAT or any other $NP-complete$ problem be reduced to this problem in polynomial-time?

If the problem is determined to be $NP-complete$, our strategy should solve that through heuristics or approximation methods.

Now, where do our $NP-complete$ problems fall in our decision problems canvas? $NP-complete$ problems are hard, intractable problems that are part of the $NP\ class$, so these fall at the intersection of the $NP\ class$ of problems and Hard problems.

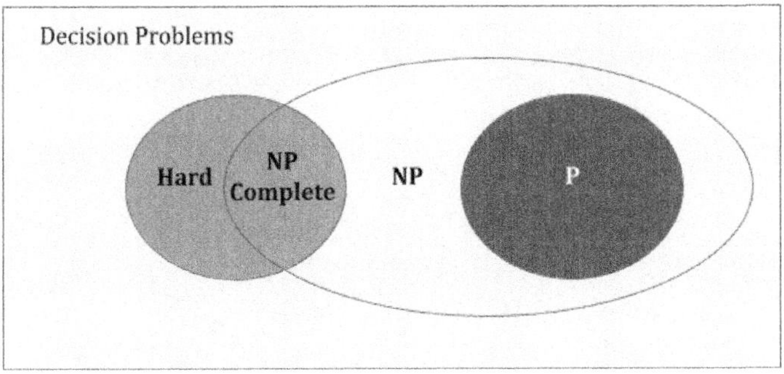

Figure 5.3.2

6. MANAGING THE UNKNOWN - PART 2

6.1 NP-Hard Problems

Let us take a moment and summarize our journey so far. The last section details how we would manage the unknown, i.e., categorize decision problems for which we have an intractable algorithm when solved using a DTM. We evolved the concept of nondeterminism and made the algorithm tractable (from a theoretical standpoint) using an NTM. A decision problem that can be solved using an NTM in polynomial-time and verified using a DTM in polynomial-time becomes part of the $NP\ class$ of problems. We went through the details of how one problem could be reduced, i.e., transformed into another problem in polynomial-time. We then established the concept of $NP - completeness$ through reducibility, and through the idea of $NP - completeness$, we identified and categorized the hardest problems in the $NP\ class$. We also learned about the discovery of the first $NP - complete$ problem, i.e., SAT, and expanded $NP - completeness$ into a class of problems.

So far, though we have not successfully identified polynomial-time algorithms (using a DTM) for many decision problems, through reducibility and $NP - completeness$, we have arrived at a solid framework to structure our research and analysis of intractable problems. But we know that intractable problems are only a subset of the problems we had initially considered hard. In our category of hard decision problems, we also included unsolved and undecidable problems. Compared to unsolved and undecidable problems, we are slightly better off with the intractable ones; at least there is an algorithm. If that is the case, could we say that the other hard problems (undecidable and unsolved) are as hard as the $NP - complete$ problems? We have to be careful about making such a statement. We can say that problem A is as hard as problem B if only a solution to A (when solved) helps us find a solution to B. In other words, we should reduce problem B to problem A in polynomial-time. Remember, until now, we have only dealt with reducibility among problems in the $NP\ class$. To generalize reducibility and include problems outside the $NP\ class$ would introduce a complication. What is the complication? The Turing machines we have designed so far, i.e., NTM and DTM, can only handle the $NP\ class$ problems, as evident through the solver depicted in Figure 6.1.1.

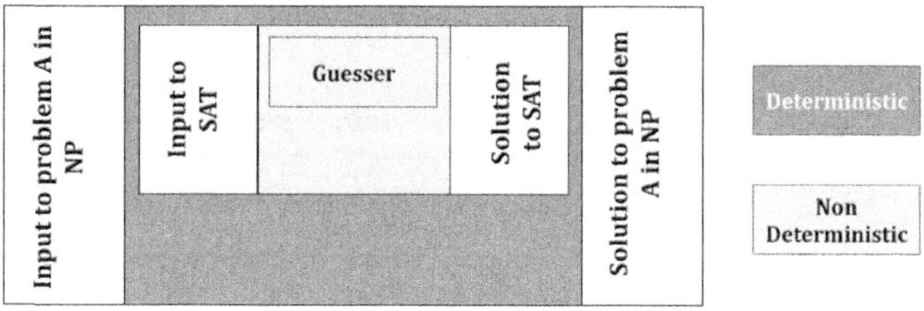

Figure 6.1.1

Therefore, before we generalize reduction, we must first evolve our Turing Machine beyond DTM and NTM. This section is about designing that newer variant of the Turing Machine that will allow us to deal with problems outside of the $NP\ class$. Our aspiration in this section would be to go beyond $NP - completeness$ and classify a problem set as hard as the hardest problems we have discussed so far. In other words, our pursuit would be to identify a problem set that includes problems that are as hard as the $NP - Complete$ problems.

Before we design our new variant of the Turing machine, let us for a moment think about how we intend to benefit through reduction. As it might be evident through Figure 6.1.1, our motivation to reduce one problem to the other, say Graph Coloring problem to SAT, is to use the solver of SAT to solve the Graph Coloring problem.

Given the above, wouldn't it be reasonable for our new variant of the Turing machine to include a component that we could call as a *subroutine*? If so, what should that component be capable of doing? Remember, we are now dealing with both problems in the $NP\ class$ and problems outside of the $NP\ class$. Therefore, the component should be capable of solving both. The next question is, how do we design this component? Developing such a component is beyond our present abilities when we do not have a way to solve the problems we expect this component to solve.

If we cannot design, how shall we proceed? Like we did earlier (for nondeterminism) when we lack a particular ability, we shall believe that we will acquire that ability in the future. Until then, we shall supplement that ability through a black box. In NTM, our black box was a guesser, but in this scenario, the black box is the component we deliberated on in the earlier paragraph. The black box is an *Oracle* that can solve a hard decision problem in polynomial-time. We could call the Oracle as a subroutine.

This variant of the Turing Machine, attached to an Oracle, is called the *Oracle Turing Machine* (*OTM*). Figure 6.1.2 shows the conceptual representation of a solver that leverages an OTM. In the following few chapters, we shall understand the design of OTM and devise algorithms to solve known $NP - complete$ problems.

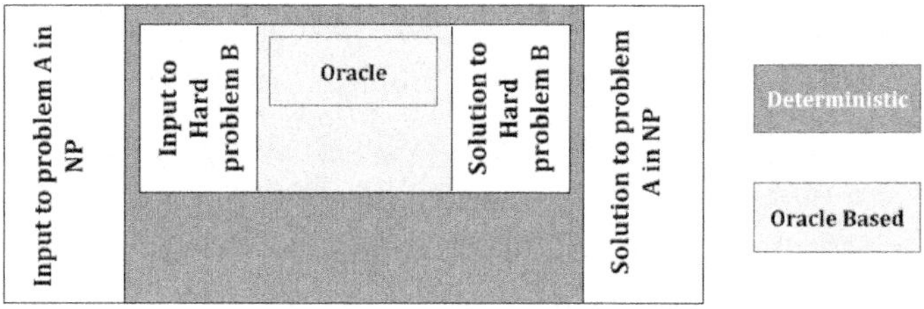

Figure 6.1.2

To stay clear, our motivation to design the OTM is not to solve hard decision problems but to explore the relationship between these intractable problems of the $NP\ class$ and hard decision problems that lie outside of $NP\ class$.

How do we explore that relationship? We shall do that by devising algorithms that solve $NP - complete$ problems (say problem A), leveraging solutions provided by Oracle to hard decision problems (say problem B) that lie outside of the $NP\ class$.

When we devise such an algorithm, we can say problem A is Turing reduced to problem B, and we can group the two problems, i.e., under the same classification. We call it *Turing Reduction* (and not reduction) because we use OTM and not our regular DTM to perform the reduction.

6.2 Oracle Turing Machine

APIfication is one of the many popular trends in computing in the twenty-first century. What does it mean? APIfication offers a specific functionality as a service for other systems to use. In essence, an *API* or an *Application Program Interface* abstracts the service's implementation details and offers a simplified interface for the consumer. The service consumer would not need to worry about how the API functions. The consumer would only care about the input structure (aka *request*) expected by the API and knowledge to parse the output (aka *response*) produced by the API.

Toward the end of the previous chapter, we articulated the motivation and the purpose of an Oracle Turing Machine, which is to devise algorithms that solve $NP - complete$ problems, leveraging solutions to hard decision problems outside the $NP\ class$. The Oracle makes the solution possible to solve hard decision problems in polynomial-time. The OTM can invoke the Oracle as a subroutine. Think of an OTM as a DTM augmented with the ability to consult the Oracle through an API. An API takes an input and returns a specific output to the caller without exposing its processing logic. Similarly, the Oracle accepts an input value and returns the solution through the *Oracle Tape*. Here is a schematic representation of an Oracle Turing Machine[8].

[8] The schematic representation of the OTM and the formal definition is as per the articulation of Michael R. Garey and David S. Johnson in the book Computers and Intractability.

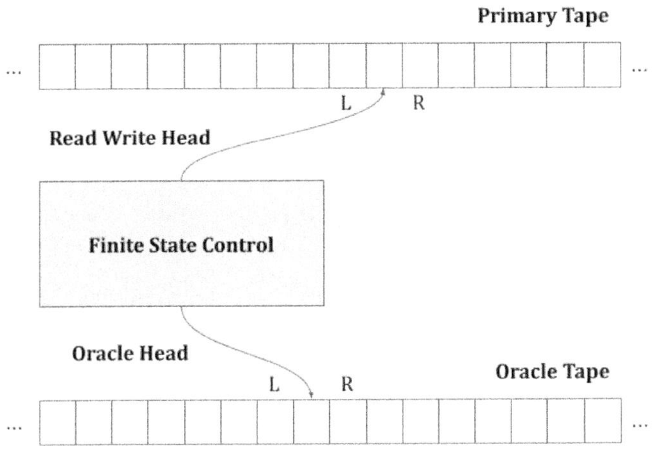

Figure 6.2.1

The Oracle Turing Machine behaves like the DTM but with a few differences, which we have captured below. A quick rehash of the properties of a DTM as articulated in Model spec 2.4.1 will be helpful.

1. A basic version of DTM, i.e., a one-tape DTM, has one tape (called primary tape) with a read-write head managed by the state transition function or the state control. However, the basic version of an OTM has an additional tape, i.e., an Oracle tape. The Oracle tape acts as the API to the Oracle to solve a hard problem in polynomial-time, i.e., $O(1)$ time. Through the Oracle tape, the Oracle accepts its input and shares the output.
2. In the DTM, the machine's state is determined based on the symbol read from the Primary tape. However,

in the case of an OTM, the machine's state is determined based on the symbols read from both the Primary Tape and the Oracle Tape.

3. Remember, our motivation for the OTM is to solve a problem using the solution to a hard problem solved by Oracle. For the OTM to invoke the Oracle as a subroutine, the machine would need to prepare the input for the Oracle to consume. Therefore, while the DTM can write to the primary tape, the OTM needs to write to the Oracle and the Primary tape.
4. The DTM has a set of finite states, out of which one would be the initial state (q_0), and some would be the final states (F). In the case of OTM, apart from the initial and final states, we would have a couple of special states—*Oracle states* q_c and q_r. When an OTM reaches state q_c, it indicates a call to the Oracle. The Oracle picks up what is available in the Oracle Tape, solves the problem, and writes back the solution to the Oracle tape. Once the Oracle completes writing the solution to the Oracle tape, the machine's state turns to q_r. The machine then resumes its operation, i.e., state transition continues as articulated in point number 2.

More formally, we may define an OTM as the following nine-tuple[9]—{Q, τ , I, ƀ, q_0, F, q_c, q_r, δ}.

[9] The schematic representation of the OTM and the formal definition is as per the articulation of Michael R. Garey and David S. Johnson in the book Computers and Intractability.

1. Q is a set of states.
2. τ is a set of tape symbols.
3. I is the set of input symbols that belong to the alphabet $I \subseteq \tau$.
4. $\flat \in \tau$ and is in τ – I, which is the special symbol (blank).
5. $q_0 \in Q$ is the initial state.
6. $F \subseteq Q$ is the set of final states.
7. $q_c \in Q$ is a special state when the Oracle is consulted.
8. $q_r \in Q$ is a special state when the Oracle responds and the machine resumes its operation.
9. δ is a transition function that maps a subset of $(Q-\{q_f, q_c\})$ X τ X τ to Q X τ X τ X {L, R, S} X {L, R, S} where $q_f \in F$.

Model Spec 6.2.1

As you might observe, the OTM differs from the DTM in Points 7, 8, and 9. Apart from the special states designated as initial and final states in a DTM, the OTM has two additional states, one to call the Oracle (q_c) and the other to resume computation (q_r). The crucial difference lies in the transition function δ, elaborated below.

1. The transitions are specified from all states besides the final states ($q_f \in F$) and when the Oracle is consulted, i.e., q_c.
2. The next state is determined based on the current state, and the symbol read in the Oracle and the Primary tape.

3. The transition includes the new symbol optionally written in both the tapes and the heads' movement, i.e., the head for the Oracle and the Primary tape.

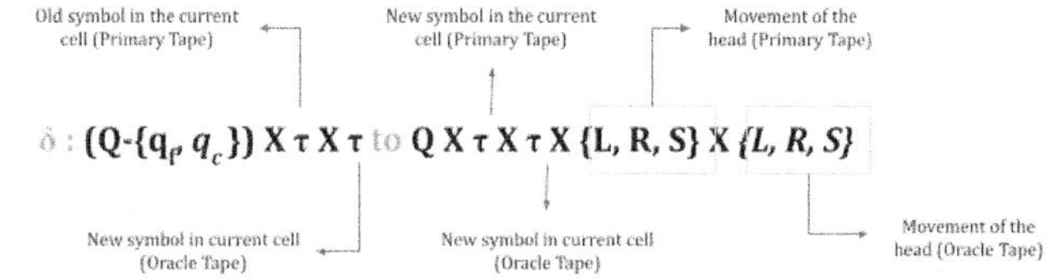

Model Spec 6.2.2 [Dissecting the Transition Function of the OTM]

In the next chapter, we shall put the construct of the OTM into action. We shall take an $NP - complete$ problem, and using an OTM, we shall (Turing) reduce that to a hard decision problem outside the $NP\ class$. In other words, we shall devise an algorithm that will solve the $NP - complete$ problem using the solution (provided by Oracle) to the hard decision problem.

6.3 Turing Reducibility

Before we put the OTM to test a real decision problem and explore the relationship between problems in the $NP\ class$ and outside of the $NP\ class$, we need to be clear of a subtle aspect about measuring algorithm efficiency. As we had learned earlier, an algorithm's efficiency reflects the resources, primarily the time in the form of state transitions the algorithm requires relative to the input size to solve the decision problem. The rate at which the resource needs grow for every increment to the input size determines whether the algorithm is tractable.

The question is, how do we determine the size of the input for a specific problem? So far, we have seen two $NP-complete$ problems—TSP and N-Queens. In the case of the TSP, the size of the input is the number of cities. In the case of the N-Queen problem, the input size is the number of queens. In both the scenarios, the input is a set, i.e., a set of cities for TSP and a set of queen pieces in the case of the N-Queens problem. When we say the best algorithms for these problems take $O(2^n)$ time, n corresponds to the input size.

What about decision problems where the input is not an array but a string? In that case, the input size would be the length of the string. An example of this is our first decision problem, where we tried to identify whether a given string is a palindrome. Our palindrome solver algorithm had a complexity[10] $O(n^2)$ when solved using a DTM. Here is a summary of the three decision problems.

Decision problem	Complexity	What is n?	Algorithm Complexity
TSP— Is there a tour across n cities less than distance d?	$O(2^n)$	Number of cities	NP (Exponential)
N-Queens problem—Can you place N queen pieces in an N × N chessboard such that no two queens attack each other?	$O(2^n)$	Number of queen pieces	NP (Exponential)
Palindrome check—Is the given string a palindrome or not?	$O(n^2)$ (on a single tape Turing machine)	Length of the input string	P (Polynomial)

Table 6.3.1

What about decision problems where the input is not a string but a number Z (with m digits) and whose algorithm relies on the value Z and not the input size, i.e., m. An excellent example of such a decision problem is the *primality test*, i.e., checking whether the given number is prime? A naive algorithm to check whether a number Z is prime is to verify

[10] There are more efficient algorithms for the palindrome solver on a multitape Turing machine.

whether Z is divisible by any of the following numbers—$\{2,3,4....\sqrt{Z}\}$. If Z is divisible by any of them, it is not a prime number. In other words, the algorithm requires approximately $\sqrt{Z}$ iterations of dividing Z. What is the efficiency of such a naive algorithm? We know that $\sqrt{Z}$ grows much slower than Z, i.e., for every unit increase to Z, we would not require more than one additional iteration because when Z increases by 1, the value of $\sqrt{Z}$ does not increase by more than 1. For instance, $\sqrt{100}$ is 10, $\sqrt{101}$ is 10.04, and $\sqrt{102}$ is 10.09. Does this mean this algorithm would complete in polynomial time and the primality test problem belongs to $P class$?

We cannot say that yet. Remember, the complexity of an algorithm is a function of the size of the input value and not the actual value. Instead of checking for the growth of $\sqrt{Z}$ for every unit increase to Z, we should check for the growth of $\sqrt{Z}$ for a unit increase to the length of Z. To see the difference clearly, we shall construct a small working table (Table 6.3.2). In that table, we shall take different values of m, i.e., lengths of numbers, and build the biggest number we can form with as many digits.

Let us consider those numbers to be Z, and through that, we shall see the implications of $\sqrt{Z}$. It might be clear that for a unit increase to the length of Z, $\sqrt{Z}$ grows much faster. Between 9 and 99 (unit increase to the length), $\sqrt{Z}$ grows from 3 to 9.95, and from 99 to 999, $\sqrt{Z}$ grows to 31.61. We see that $\sqrt{Z}$ = $2^{log(n)}$, which is exponential. Thus, the algorithm for primality testing is exponential and is on the order of $2^{log(n)}$, i.e., $O(2^{log(n)})$.

Number of Digits (m)	Maximum number with m digits (Z)	$\sqrt{Z}$ rounded* (n)	log(n)*
1	9	3.00	1.58
2	99	9.95	3.31
3	999	31.61	4.98
4	9999	99.99	6.64
5	99999	316.23	8.30
6	999999	1000.00	9.97
7	9999999	3162.28	11.63
8	99999999	10000.00	13.29
...	...	...	...

* rounded to two decimals

Table 6.3.2

Algorithms of this kind, i.e., those that appear to belong to the P $class$ based on the value of the input (Z) but are intractable (in some cases unsolvable) based on the length of the input, are categorized as *Pseudo Polynomial time* (PP) algorithms.

Here is the updated version of the table with details of Primality testing included.

Decision problem	Complexity	What is n?	Algorithm Complexity
TSP— Is there a tour across n cities less than distance d?	$O(2^n)$	Number of cities	NP (Exponential)
N-Queens problem—Can you place N queen pieces in an N × N chessboard such that no two queens attack each other?	$O(2^n)$	Number of queen pieces	NP (Exponential)
Palindrome check—Is the given string a palindrome or not?	$O(n^2)$ (on a single tape Turing machine)	Length of the input string	P (Polynomial)
Primality test—Is the given number Z prime?	$2^{log(n)}$ (naive method)	The square root of the input number	NP (Exponential) and PP (Pseudo Polynomial)

Table 6.3.3

The question in your mind is likely to be—why did we have to recap and clarify this aspect (pseudo polynomial-time) of algorithm efficiency now? Wasn't our plan to design a solver for a decision problem using an OTM? We took the trouble of understanding Pseudo polynomial-time because the hard decision problem that we are about to leverage in our OTM has Pseudo Polynomial-time complexity.

We now have all the knowledge to design our first solver using OTM. The decision problem that we shall solve is the *Partition problem* (an $NP-complete$ problem), and to solve that, we shall use the solver of a hard problem—the Kth *Largest Subset problem.* Figure 6.3.1 captures the conceptual view of our Partition problem solver.

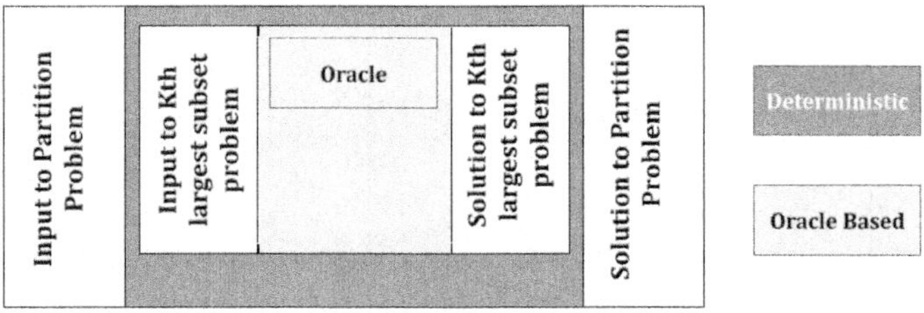

Figure 6.3.1

Let us start with understanding both the problems in detail.

Partition Problem: Given a set S of numbers, can S be partitioned into two sets A and A' such that they both are of the same size, i.e., s(A) = s(A')? We shall define the size of a set as the sum of all its elements through the below formula.

$$s(A) = \sum_{a \in A} a$$

For instance, S={1,2,3} can be partitioned with A={1,2} and A'={3}, whereas set S={1,2,4} cannot be partitioned. Partition problem is an $NP-complete$ problem.

K^{th} Largest Subset problem: Given a set S of numbers and two integers B and K, can there be at least K subsets $A' \subseteq A$ that satisfy the condition $s(A') <= B$?

For instance, given a set S={1,2,3} and B=3, the above statement is true for K<=5. In other words, the largest number of subsets that we can form out of set S with size at most 3 is 5. The below table (Table 6.3.4) shows these five subsets in bold.

$A' \subseteq A$	$s(A')$
{}	**0**
{1}	**1**
{2}	**2**
{3}	**3**
{1,2}	**3**
{1,3}	4
{2,3}	5
{1,2,3}	6

Table 6.3.4

The input to the Kth largest subset problem are numbers K (number of subsets) and B (size of the subset). The decision problem involves identifying K subsets from set S, with each subset having a size of B. Forget about polynomial time algorithms; we don't even have a nondeterministic algorithm to solve this problem. Therefore, this problem is outside of the NP $class$.

How is this problem outside of NP $class$? After all, we have the guesser module part of the NTM. Could we not guess the solution, i.e., guess the K subsets for a given set S? Though the guesser can nondeterministically make the right choice, we should determine the list of options in polynomial-time. In this case, though K is a number, it can hold values anywhere between 0 and 2^n where n is the count of elements that makes the set S. The number of choices grows exponentially relative to the number of elements in the input set S. As seen in Table 6.3.4, for a set with three elements, K subsets have to be chosen from eight, i.e., 2^3 subsets. Hence, this problem is both Pseudo Polynomial and outside the NP $class$. We can find the algorithm[11] for solving the Partition Problem below using the Kth largest subset problem's solution.

Our strategy to solve the partition problem using the solver for the Kth largest subset problem has two steps. Let us go through each step in detail.

1. Solving the partition problem of a set S is about identifying at least two subsets that are half the size of the original set S. Therefore, for a set to be partitionable, its size, i.e., $s(S)$ needs to be an even

[11] The Kth largest subset problem got classified NP-hard when Johnson and Kashdan (in 1976) Turing-reduced the Partition Problem to the Kth largest subset problem.

number. If $s(S)$ is an odd number, we can straight away decide that the set cannot be partitioned.

2. Now, if $s(S)$ is even, we move to the second step. We calculate half the value of $s(S)$ and look for one subset in S of size $\frac{s(S)}{2}$. Why only one subset? If we can find one subset (say A) that is half the size of the original set S then there is another subset with $S-A$ elements that is also half the size of set S. We identify that first subset by leveraging the solver of the Kth largest subset problem. We arrive at the first partition through the following steps.

    a. A set S with n elements can have 2^n possible subsets. Our first task would be to find the least number of subsets with a size of at most $\frac{s(S)}{2}$. To do this, we shall apply the binary search technique, which we briefly reviewed in Chapter 3.1. We shall call the solver for the Kth largest subset problem n times for different values of K. We shall start with a window defined by two variables, namely, Kmin and Kmax.

    Kmin = 0, i.e., minimum number of subsets

    Kmax = 2^n, i.e., the maximum number of subsets

Through the solver for the Kth largest subset, equating K to (Kmin +Kmax)/2, we check for the existence of at least K subsets of size $\frac{s(S)}{2}$. Based on the solver's result, we shrink the window to the right (set Kmin to the midpoint value K) or the left (set Kmax to the midpoint value K). We then call the solver for the Kth largest subset with the recalculated value of K. Eventually, after n steps, we shall arrive at a value of K that will equal the least number of subsets with a size of at most $\frac{s(S)}{2}$.

b. The final value of K arrived in the earlier step indicates that at least K subsets have a size of at most $\frac{s(S)}{2}$. How could we know if one of those subsets is of size $\frac{s(S)}{2}$? We can do that by calling the Kth largest subset problem one more time. This time, our pursuit would be to check for the existence of at least K subsets that have the size of at most $\frac{s(S)}{2} - 1$, i.e., one less than half the size of S. If we succeed in that check, then we have at least K subsets that have a size of at most $\frac{s(S)}{2} - 1$ which would mean there never was a partition of size $\frac{s(S)}{2}$. A failure in the last step would suggest we have found our first partition of size $\frac{s(S)}{2}$ and solved the partition problem.

The pseudo-code for the above algorithm is shared below.

```
# Initialize the solver for the partition problem.
# The solver takes an input set S with a set of finite numbers.
# The solver returns true if the input set is partitionable and
# returns false otherwise.
# S = {s1, s2, .... sn }.

Is_Set_Partitionable(S):

        # Count the number of elements in set S
        Set_Count = count(S)

        # Calculate the size of set S, i.e., calculate the sum
        # of all elements in set S
        # sum(S) = s1+ s2+...sn
        Set_Size = sum(S)

        # If the size of the set is not even, then the set
        # cannot be partitioned.
        If Set_Size % 2 == 1:
                Return(0)

        # Capture the partitioned set size
        # in variable Partitioned_Set_Size
        Partitioned_Set_Size=Set_Size/2

        # Initialize the window
        K_min = 0
        K_max = 2^Set_Count

        # Begin loop
        i_loop=0
        While i_loop < Set_Count:
```

```
        If (K_max - K_min == 1):

                K=K_min
                break

        Else:

                K=(K_min+K_max)/2
                # The below step calls the solver of
                # the Kth largest subset problem.
                # The solver through the help of the
                # Oracle returns true or false
                # Solver returns true if K subsets
                # are found
                # sized Partitioned_Set_Size
                # Solver returns false otherwise

                i_check= Find_K_LargestSubset(S,
                Partitioned_Set_Size, K)

                If i_check == true:
                        K_min = K
                Else:
                        K_max = K

        i_loop = i_loop+1

    # The below step calls the solver of the Kth largest
    # subset problem
    # Find presence of the K largest subsets with size 1
    # less than Partitioned_Set_Size
    i_check1=                    Find_K_LargestSubset(S,
    Partitioned_Set_Size-1, K)

    # Return true if the set is determined to be
    # partitionable
```

```
If K >0 and i_check != i_check1:
        Return true
Else:
        Return false
```

Algorithm 6.3.1

Leaving aside the step to call the solver, i.e., Find_K_LargestSubset, the above algorithm's remaining steps have a Polynomial-time complexity. By solving the Partition Problem using the Oracle-based solver of a Kth largest Subset problem, what we have done is (Turing) reduced an $NP - complete$ problem to a hard problem outside of the $NP\ class$. Not only the Kth largest Subset problem but there are also other hard problems to which $NP - complete$ problems could be reduced to. We shall formally categorize all such decision problems as $NP - hard$ problems, and this will be the last category of problems that we shall capture in our decision canvas.

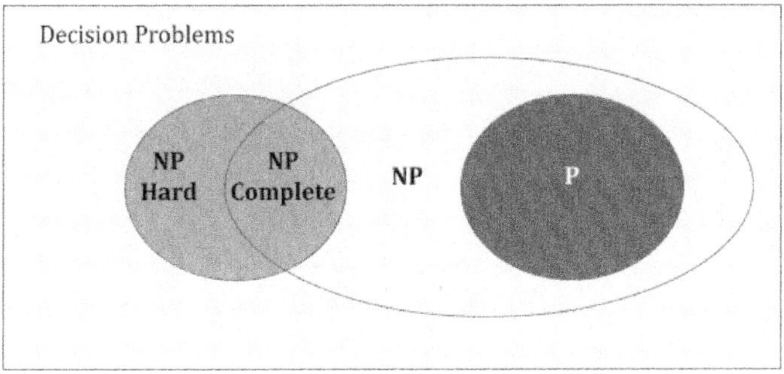

Figure 6.3.2

The classification of $NP - hard$ problems includes all problems as hard as the hardest problems in the $NP\ class$.

But this definition holds good to every $NP - complete$ problem too. Every $NP - complete$ problem can be reduced to SAT, and SAT is one of the hardest problems in the $NP\ class$. Therefore, the category of $NP - hard$ problems includes both $NP - complete$ problems and hard problems (unsolvable and undecidable) to which $NP - complete$ problems could be Turing reduced to.

7. SUMMARY

7.1 Million Dollar Problem—P vs. NP

We have classified all decision problems (that we are aware of) into four categories. With that classification and their relationships, we have the necessary foundation to understand the million-dollar question—*What is the P vs. NP Problem?* Let us quickly summarize the four classifications of problems. It might be easier to understand the motivation for each class and their relationships through the following sequence. The emergence of each class is an attempt to either know the unknown or manage the unknown that existed in the earlier classification.

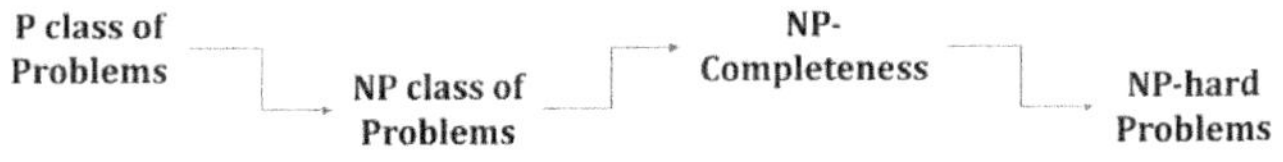

Figure 7.1.1

P class: These are the class of decision problems for which we have an algorithm that can take a *reasonable amount* of time when solved using a Turing Machine. By reasonable amount of time, we mean algorithms that can complete in polynomial-time using a DTM.

NP class: These class of problems emerged when we stumbled upon decision problems, for which the best algorithms took an unreasonable amount of time using a DTM. In other words, such problems did not have a polynomial-time algorithm using a DTM. Those problems were considered intractable. We did our first abstraction by introducing the concept of Nondeterminism and the NTM. An NTM is a DTM augmented with a guessing module. Intractable problems for which we could devise algorithms with the following characteristics got classified under the $NP\ class$ of problems:

- Solvable in polynomial-time using an NTM
- Verifiable in polynomial-time using a DTM

NP-completeness: If the $NP\ class$ of problems helped us package the unknown through the concept of nondeterminism, $NP - completeness$ was our pursuit of managing that unknown. We accomplished that through the reduction process, which involved transforming one NP class problem to another in the $NP\ class$ in polynomial-time. Through reduction, we intended to identify one master problem or a set of master problems to which all other problems in the $NP\ class$ could be reduced to (in polynomial-time). This way, we could spend our energies on solving a few intractable decision problems. We classified such decision problems as $NP - complete$ problems, and informally, they were also the hardest problems in the $NP\ class$.

NP-hard: Through $NP - completeness$, we were only able to classify intractable problems. What about decision problems that are either undecidable or unsolved, i.e., problems outside of the $NP\ class$? Is there a way to relate them with $NP - complete$ problems? Here is where we performed our second abstraction through the concept of Turing Reduction and introduced the OTM (Oracle Turing

Machine). Using an OTM, we understood how $NP-complete$ problems could be Turing reduced in polynomial-time to problems outside of the $NP\ class$, thus proving these hard problems that lie outside of the $NP\ class$ are as hard as the hardest problems that lie inside the $NP\ class$. In other words, $NP-hard$ problems are as hard as $NP-Complete$ problems. We shall capture the classification of decision problems in our canvas for one last time.

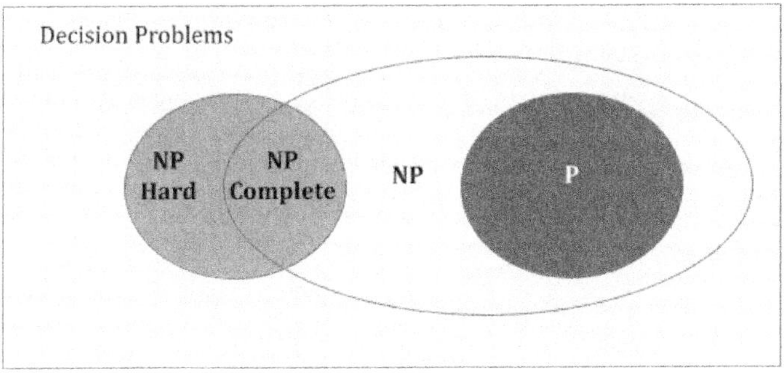

Figure 7.1.2

Therefore, what is the $P\ vs. NP\ Problem$, and why is it important? Let us recall the first abstraction introduced through nondeterminism and the guessing module to answer that. The concept of nondeterminism is relevant because we do not have tractable algorithms for certain decision problems. The moment we solve one of the $NP-complete$ problems in polynomial-time (using a DTM), then the concept of nondeterminism will no longer be relevant as the entire class of NP would collapse into the $P\ class$ problems, i.e., $P\ would\ be\ the\ same\ as\ NP\ or\ P=NP$.

The point is, does that possibility exist? Do we have a chance of solving any $NP-complete$ decision problem in polynomial-time using a DTM? Here is the interesting part; so far, mathematicians worldwide have not been able to prove (that such a possibility exists) nor disprove (that it doesn't exist), thus keeping the question $(Is\,P=NP?)$ open.

What do $NP-hard$ problems tell us? Because every $NP-hard$ Problem is a reduced version, i.e., Turing reduced version of some $NP-complete$ problem, solving an $NP-Hard$ problem in polynomial-time (using a DTM) is equivalent to proving that $P=NP$. In other words, unless $P\,equals\,NP$, we don't stand a chance to solve any of the $NP-hard$ problems in polynomial-time (using a DTM).

Why would the $P\,vs.NP\,Problem$ or the question $Is\,P=NP?$ such a big deal? What warrants it to be a million-dollar question? The answer lies in the consequences we will have to face when we find an answer to this question.

Though not mathematically proven, the general belief is that $P\neq NP$. American Computer scientist William Gasarch had conducted multiple surveys among computer theorists on what they believed to be the solution to the problem. The survey results indicate a steady increase in the confidence that $P\neq NP$ over the past few decades. As of 2019, 88 percent of computer theorists believed that $P\neq NP$. Though this question has been unanswered since the 1970s, many have started to bet on the possibility of $P\neq NP$. A classic example is the implementation of data security through RSA cryptosystem, which is foundational to the way we transact over the Internet. The strength of the RSA cryptosystem lies in the difficulty of identifying the prime factors of a large number. Identifying prime factors of a number is an $NP - complete$ problem. RSA's cryptosystems are effective today because there is no polynomial-time algorithm to solve the same problem. Imagine the current setup's possibilities to a hacker when it gets proven that $P = NP$.

If the above scenario was from a data security standpoint, let us look at its impact from a philosophical angle. For a moment, imagine a world where P gets proven to be the same as NP, i.e., $P = NP$. Now, think about a scenario where you sit with your friend to play your favorite board game, and your friend has access to a solver for the same. Now, how interesting would that game be? Remember, we have proved that P is equal to NP in that world. The solver for the board problem would be far more effective, be accurate, and, more importantly, provide deterministic results to the problem. You might think we do have solvers for those board games (or $NP - complete$ problems) today too, but the difference is today's solvers of $NP - complete$ problems are still an implementation of somebody's idea. None of the solvers that exist today are complete solutions. They either apply clever heuristics or approximations to provide results that we can put to practical use. We wouldn't require such techniques in a world where P is equal to NP. In such a world, we would build solvers that would arrive at an effective solution in polynomial-time by trying out all possible paths in a solution tree. Scott Anderson, an American Computer scientist, beautifully summed up life in that scenario through his following words:

If P = NP, then the world would be a profoundly different place than we usually assume it to be. There would be no special value in "creative leaps" and no fundamental gap between solving a problem and recognizing the solution once it's found.

Before we wrap up, another important fact is to know how these terminologies emerged. In the book, Computer Algorithms and Intractability, authors Michael R Gary & David S. Johnson describe the history behind these terms, primarily $NP - complete$ and $NP - hard$. American Computer scientist Donald Knuth is credited for formalizing these terminologies among researchers and mathematicians in the 1970s. The formalization also involved conducting many surveys among researchers worldwide.

7.2 Role of Quantum Computers

In October 2019, Google's CEO Sundar Pichai revealed that the research team at Google had achieved a significant milestone, which he claimed to be the *Hello World* moment in *Quantum Computing*. It was the moment the world had been waiting for. With the help of its Quantum Computer, Sycamore, Google performed a calculation in 200 seconds that would have taken the world's fastest *Classical Computer* (aka supercomputer) 10,000 years to complete. A Classical Computer is the one we all use today, built on the concepts of a Turing Machine. Though Sundar Pichai clarified that we are still in the initial days of Quantum Computing and the problem solved by Sycamore had little practical application, the fact remains, both interest and progress in Quantum Computing have seen a steady rise in the past few decades.

While an in-depth study of Quantum Computing is well beyond this book's scope, what we shall explore in this chapter is the motivation for Quantum Computing and how it differed from the motivations for a Classical Computer. We shall also clarify certain misconceptions about Quantum Computers, especially around their perceived similarity with NTM, and, most importantly, explore its relevance to the problems we have classified as hard decision problems. In other words, we would attempt to answer the question—*Can Quantum Computers help solve any of the decision problems that we have classified as NP-hard or NP-complete?*

During the early nineteenth century, the word computer would typically refer to a human who would do computational tasks. A machine that did computational tasks was called a digital computer back then. Now, how does a human compute? A human is likely to use a pen and paper, follow some steps, remember a few details, and complete the computation. As conceived by Alan Turing, the notion of a computer, what we now call the Turing machine, was inspired by how humans performed computation. The pen is the Turing machine's head, the paper is the tape, and the process and the steps we remember are the state relation. While the idea of a Turing Machine did capture the imagination of most mathematicians and computer scientists around the world, it did not convince everyone, especially physicists. Let us see why.

Turing machine is a mathematician's pursuit of arriving at a universal computing machine capable of simulating a computation method as performed by a human. On the other hand, the model of a Quantum Computer[12] is a physicist's pursuit of arriving at a universal computing device, which can efficiently simulate other physical systems. What do we mean by a physical system, and why would we simulate one? Could we not do that using a classical computer even if we had to? Let us think about the scenario of a pharma company that intends to discover a vaccine for a pandemic like the Covid-19. Such research is going to involve complex computations and simulations involving molecular study. If a

[12] Quantum Computing for the very curious (https://quantum.country/qcvc)

4×4 sudoku problem requires hundreds of Boolean variables only to encode the problem, imagine the number of Boolean variables that we would need to encode (forget processing for now) complex molecules with hundreds or thousands of atoms. The count would explode exponentially and quickly make the computation too complicated when solved using a classical computer.

What is the source for such complexity? The foundational building block of information in a classical computer is a *bit*. A bit is nothing but an electric charge preserved in a capacitor that we can manipulate, i.e., turn it off or on (0 or 1). Every information, ranging from alphabets, numbers, or molecular structure that we would want the classical computer to store and process, encodes 0s and 1s. As information gets complex, its encoding gets complex too.

What's different with a Quantum Computer? Instead of a bit, the foundational building block of a Quantum computer is a *qubit*. You could think of a qubit as the state of the electron that is boxed inside a semiconductor. There are two possible states for an electron to be in—spin-up and spin-down states. Just like the way we would manipulate a bit, we could manipulate a qubit too. The only difference is that unlike the bit of a classical machine that can either be in state 0 or 1, the qubit's state will not be deterministic. The qubit will be in spin-up and spin-down states simultaneously, each with a certain amount of probability. This lack of determinism does not mean a Quantum computer is an NTM. In an NTM, what remains nondeterministic is how the guesser makes the right choice in $O(1)$ time. After making a choice, the NTM arrives at one of the many states. However, in the case of a Quantum Machine, a qubit can be in more than one state simultaneously. This phenomenon is called *superposition*, and this is a fundamental principle of Quantum Mechanics.

At an atomic or subatomic scale, every physical system (or matter) is subjected to rules of Quantum Mechanics. From that standpoint, the physicist's perspective is that, compared to bits, qubits are naturally suited to capture the physical properties of an atom. With the ability to manipulate these qubits, Quantum Computers can be far more efficient in simulating other physical systems, which are proven hard to be solved using a classical computer.

Besides molecular simulations, how good are Quantum Computers in solving problems that classical computers find hard to solve? There are two exciting quantum algorithms devised so far, and we shall look into both of them. Before we discuss them, let us understand a critical difference between the results delivered by a quantum algorithm and its classical equivalent. As a qubit can be in multiple states of different probabilities, the results produced by quantum algorithms are probabilistic. For instance, when a classical computer executes an algorithm to solve a particular problem, say searching for a specific string in a database, irrespective of whether the string was present in the database, the result would have a probability of 1. In other words, according to the classical computer, the string was either present or not present. However, a Quantum search algorithm, the first quantum algorithm that we will explore in this chapter, would find an input string's presence (or absence) with a certain probability.

In 1996, Lov Kumar Grover, an Indian American computer scientist, devised an important quantum algorithm to search in an unstructured database. This algorithm is also known as *Grover's algorithm.* An unstructured database is one where data is not indexed. The most efficient algorithm (on a classical computer) that we have today has an efficiency $O(log(n))$ on structured data and an efficiency $O(n)$ on unstructured data. Grover's quantum algorithm can perform such a search on an unstructured database with an efficiency $O(\sqrt{n})$ with a high probability, of course.

With an efficiency $O(\sqrt{n})$, Grover's Quantum algorithm provides a quadratic speedup compared to its classical equivalent. As you might have noticed by now, search by itself is not a hard problem, i.e., classical computers can perform a search in polynomial-time. Do we have quantum algorithms to solve hard problems, i.e., problems for which we do not have a polynomial-time algorithm (using a DTM) yet? The answer is yes, which brings us to our second quantum algorithm.

The most famous quantum algorithm that we have to date is Shor's Algorithm to solve integer factorization. This Quantum algorithm was invented by an American mathematician, Peter Shor, in the year 1994. *Shor's algorithm* can perform integer factorization in polynomial-time. Unlike Grover's algorithm, Shor's algorithm is exponentially faster when compared to its classical counterpart. Here again, Shor's algorithm will provide the results with a high level of certainty, i.e., a probability score of more than $\frac{2}{3}$.

If quantum algorithms are far more efficient than their classical counterparts, could Quantum Computers be deployed to solve real-world hard problems today? Here is the catch. There is little doubt that Quantum Computing has seen phenomenal progress over the past few decades, and it continues to grab more and more mindshare every day. Yet, the fact is that we are still in the initial days of Quantum Computing. The most sophisticated Quantum Machines that we have today can handle a few dozens of qubits only. For instance, Google's sycamore processor that we referred to at the beginning of this chapter can handle fifty-three qubits. We are a long way away from Quantum Computers that are portable, scalable, and fault-tolerant. In 2020, IBM announced its plan to build the first 1000-qubit Quantum Computer in 2023. The question of whether Quantum Computers would replace classical computers in the future? That is an interesting one, maybe for another book.

8. APPENDIX

8.1 The Halting Problem

This chapter is a dedication to the genius of Alan Turing. Among all hard decision problems, the *Halting Problem* holds a special place. Though the term $NP - hard$ was coined much later, the Halting Problem is the first $NP - hard$ problem discovered. It also holds a historical significance, as it was through this problem that Alan Turing convinced the world that Hilbert's framework was untenable. How did Turing do that? Through a logical thought experiment, Turing showed that this problem is ***undecidable*** and made it clear that there are some decision problems whose solutions are beyond the grasp of the human mind. This idea stood in direct contrast with the belief held by prominent mathematicians, especially David Hilbert, who believed we could know everything about this world through math. This chapter is about that thought experiment.

Let us start with the definition of the Halting Problem—Halting Problem is the decision problem of determining if a computer program for a specific input will complete its execution or run forever. The input is the data or information required for processing by the program. In the Traveling Salesman decision problem, the input is the list of cities, distances across pairs of cities, and the total tour distance we want the algorithm to compare. Alan Turing proved that we could not write a general algorithm that can decide if any given program and its input can complete its execution in a finite number of steps. Turing's proof is clever, and he does that through a thought experiment.

The thought experiment begins with an assumption that the solution to the Halting problem exists, i.e., we have a program P that accepts any other program P' as input and can decide if its input program P' can complete in finite steps. The point to note here is that the input to our program P is another program. Now that we have program P, let us construct another program Q that does the exact opposite of what P decides, i.e., if P decides that P' halts, then Q runs forever. If P decides that P' will run forever, Q will halt.

The logic of a program running forever can be easily designed through an infinite loop captured inside a condition that always returns true. We could implement it in a high-level programming language through the following line of code. In a Turing Machine, we can realize this through a state transition where the source and the target state are the same upon encountering any character in the tape.

$$while\ True:$$

Here comes the genius of Turing. What if we choose to give program Q (instead of P') as input to program P? Remember, program Q is expected to do the opposite of what program P decides about Q, i.e., if P decides that Q would halt, then Q would have to run forever. If Q runs forever, then Q is also expected to halt, i.e., do the opposite of what P decides about Q, and P would have rightly detected Q cannot halt. We have reached a contradiction that program Q will have to halt and run forever simultaneously. This contradiction concludes that our original assumption is invalid, i.e., such a program P cannot exist.

8.2 Cook-Levin Theorem

This chapter will mathematically prove Cook's theorem (also called the Cook–Levin theorem).

Theorem: Boolean Satisfiability is $NP - complete$

Before we begin that, we will do a quick recap of the anatomy of the various solvers that we have designed so far. We will take an example of the very first decision problem—the palindrome solver. The Turing machine of our palindrome solver will have the following configuration as part of the seven-tuple:

- Input string s on the tape prepared from the input symbols I.
- Head aligned to the beginning cell of the tape.
- State transition function δ.

With the above configuration, our palindrome solver will decide whether the input string on the tape is a palindrome. Suppose we define a language L as a set of all palindromes generated from the input alphabet I. In that case, we can say that our palindrome solver can accept that language L because for every string $s \in L$, when configured on the tape, our solver would be able to decide whether s is a palindrome. In the case of TSP, the language can be a set of all n cities (along with distances across each pair) that has a loop of distance d. Essentially, we can represent a decision problem P as a language L.

Now, coming back to Cook's theorem, we mean the following when we say Boolean Satisfiability is $NP - complete$:

1. Boolean Satisfiability problem belongs to $NP\ class$.
2. We can reduce every other problem in $NP\ class$ to SAT in polynomial-time. An equivalent way of saying this would be— for every NTM that accepts a language L, there is a Boolean expression that is satisfiable for all s that belong to L. The point is that Boolean expression should be encodable in polynomial-time, and the bulk of this chapter would be around proving this point.

Proving the first part of Cook's theorem is relatively straightforward. As covered in our earlier chapters, problem P would belong to the $NP\ class$ when it exhibits the following characteristics:

1. We can design a nondeterministic algorithm and solve problem P using an NTM in polynomial-time; and
2. We can verify the solution to problem P in polynomial-time using a DTM.

If the boolean expression has n variables, its length will be bound by some polynomial $p(n)$. Given that, we can arrive at the possible assignments for the n variables using an

NTM. The NTM will complete in polynomial-time (n steps, to be precise) using the guessing module. Once the guessing is complete, we will be able to perform the verification in polynomial time (using a DTM) since the length of the boolean expression is bound by $p(n)$. Thus we are able to prove that the SAT problem belongs to the *NP class*.

To prove the second part[13] of Cook's theorem, we shall be considering an NTM M with the following properties as part of its seven tuple:

1. Our Turing machine M can be in s possible states defined by $Q = \{ q_1, q_2, q_3 \dots q_s \}$.
2. We shall assume q_1 to be the initial state.
3. We shall assume q_2 to be the final state.
4. τ the set of m tape symbols defined by $\tau = \{ x_1, x_2, x_3 \dots x_m \}$. One of the symbols is the blank symbol, i.e., ƀ.
5. The transition relation δ defines the moves of the Turing machine.

To either accept or reject an input string of length n, starting from the initial state, our Turing Machine will go through a certain number of state transitions (say T) before reaching one of the final states. We have depicted this transition below.

$$Q_1 \rightarrow Q_2 \rightarrow Q_3 \rightarrow \dots Q_T$$

---

[13] Proof as articulated by Prof. Kamala Krithivasan, Department of Computer Science and Engineering, IIT Madras as part of the course Theory of Automata, Formal Languages and Computation.

As our Turing Machine is an NTM, it needs to complete in polynomial-time, i.e., the number of state transitions T has to be expressed as a polynomial and let us call it $p(n)$. To summarize, the following would hold good for the Turing machine M with the above configuration.

$$Q_1 = q_1$$
$$Q_t = q_2$$
$$T \leq p(n)$$

Just the way we laid out the rules for Sudoku and then encoded each of the rules as a Boolean expression, here too, we shall begin with laying out the rules or constraints of the Turing machine and encode the same. Our Turing machine M would be constrained by rules A through G:

A. The head can scan only one cell at any step (or time) t.
B. Each cell can contain only one symbol at any step t.
C. The state of the Turing Machine is unique for a particular step t.
D. Only the cell contents pointed by the head may change at every step.
E. A change in the Turing Machine is specified through the transition relation δ.
F. The Turing Machine begins with the Initial State—q_1.
G. The Turing Machine halts at the final state—q_2.

If we can encode each of the above rules as a Boolean expression, then the entire construct of our NTM can be expressed as one giant Boolean expression. A quick recap of the notation here—$\wedge$ denotes Boolean AND, $\vee$ denotes Boolean OR, and $\neg$ denotes Boolean NOT.

$$A \wedge B \wedge C \wedge D \wedge E \wedge F \wedge G$$

The only catch is that such an encoding should be possible in polynomial-time. If the encoding was possible in polynomial-time then we should also be able to write such an expression back to the tape in polynomial-time. In other words, for the encoding to be possible in polynomial-time, the length of the Boolean expression should be bound by a polynomial. Therefore, we shall prove the second part of Cook's theorem by mathematically deriving the length of every encoded Boolean expression corresponding to each of the seven rules (A through G) and proving that the derived length is bound by a polynomial.

To help with the encoding of the above rules, we would need to establish certain Boolean variables, and we shall go over each one of them.

1. $c_{<i,j,t>} = 1$ if the ith cell in the tape contains the jth symbol at time t (or step t).
   a. We know that there cannot be more than $p(n)$ steps. Therefore, $0 \leq t \leq p(n)$.
   b. We also know that, at every step, the head of the Turing Machine can move only one cell,

either to the right or the left, which would mean, at the max, the head of the Turing machine may explore $p(n)$ distinct cells. Therefore, $1 \leq i \leq p(n)$.

c. We also know that there can be no more than m distinct symbols read from the tape. Therefore, $1 \leq j \leq m$.

Given the above, we know the number of Boolean variables $c_{<i,j,t>}$ we would need is m times $p(n)^2$. In other words, the number of Boolean variables $c_{<i,j,t>}$ is $O(p(n)^2)$.

2. $H_{<i,t>} = 1$ if the head scans the ith cell at time t (or step t).

   Here, again, we can calculate that the number of Boolean variables $H_{<i,t>}$ that we would need is $p(n)^2$ or $O(p(n)^2)$ because both i and t can have a value between 0 and $p(n)$.

3. $S_{<k,t>} = 1$ if the state is q_k at time t (or step t).

   a. We know that there cannot be more than s states. Therefore, $1 \leq k \leq s$, and we had already calculated the range for t in Step 1. Thus, the number of Boolean variables $S_{<k,t>}$ that we would need is s times $p(n)$, which is $O(p(n))$.

Now that we have established the foundational Boolean variables, let us familiarize ourselves with the following three notations. We shall be using them extensively as we begin our encoding process.

- $\prod_{i=1}^{i=n} x_i = x_1 \wedge x_2 \wedge x_3 \ldots \wedge x_n$—All Boolean (AND) variables need to be true.
- $\sum_{i=1}^{i=n} x_i = x_1 \vee x_2 \vee x_3 \ldots \vee x_n$—At least one (OR) of the Boolean variables needs to be true.
- $x_1 \oplus x_2 \oplus x_3 \ldots \oplus x_n =$

  $(x_1 \vee x_2 \vee x_3 \ldots \vee x_n) \wedge \prod_{i \neq j} (\neg x_i \vee \neg x_j)$

  —Not more than one (exclusive OR or X-OR) of the Boolean variables needs to be true.

With the above knowledge, let us begin encoding the seven constraints or rules (A through G) that we had laid out for our Turing machine.

A: The head can scan only one cell at any step (or time) t.

Using our Boolean variable $H_{<i,t>}$, we can encode the above constraint in the following manner for a particular step.

$$A_t = H_{<1,t>} \oplus H_{<2,t>} \oplus H_{<3,t>} \ldots\ldots\ldots \oplus H_{<p(n),t>}$$

(1)

The above expression (1) can also be extended to ensure the constraint is applied for every step.

$$A = A_0 \land A_1 \land A_2 \land A_3 \land \ldots\ldots\ldots\ldots\ldots A_{p(n)} \qquad (2)$$

While we successfully encoded the constraint as a Boolean expression, we need to ensure the above encoding is possible in polynomial-time. We shall begin with dissecting the first equation, i.e., A_t .

$$A_t = (H_{<1,t>} \lor H_{<2,t>} \lor H_{<3,t>} \ldots\ldots\ldots \oplus H_{<p(n),t>}) \land$$

$$\prod_{i \neq j} (\neg H_{<i,t>} \lor \neg H_{<j,t>})$$

We can see the above equation's length bound by the second part of the equation. For every additional boolean variable $H_{<i,j>}$, to the above equation, the second part of the above equation would grow much faster than the first part. For instance, for three Boolean variables of $H_{<1,t>}$, we can split the second part of the above equation into three (2 + 1) parts. For four such Boolean variables, it will be six (3 + 2 + 1) parts, and so on. In summary, for $p(n)$ variables, there will be $1 + 2 + 3 + \ldots + (p(n) - 1)$ parts, which is $O(p(n)^2)$. Remember, this is only for a specific step. For all steps, a similar count derived from equation (2) would be $O(p(n)^3)$.

With the above, we have mathematically derived that the length of the Boolean expression encoding the first constraint A is bound by the polynomial $p(n)^3$.

B: Each cell can contain only one symbol at any step t.

If $B_{<i,t>}$ denotes the possibility that i^{th} cell in time t can have one of the m symbols then such an expression can be expressed as follows:

$$B_{<i,t>} = c_{<i,1,t>} \oplus c_{<i,2,t>} \oplus c_{<i,3,t>} \oplus \ldots c_{<i,m,t>}$$

Taking learning from our first constraint A, we can infer the length of the above expression to be bounded by m^2. But to complete encoding of our current constraint, we would need to extend the above equation for all values of i and t, i.e., we would need to encode B the following way:

$$B = \prod_{i=1,t=0}^{i,t=p(n)} B_{<i,t>}$$

With i ranging from 1 through $p(n)$ and t ranging from 0 through $p(n)$, the length of the above Boolean expression would be bound by $m^2 p(n)^2$, which is $O(p(n)^2)$, again is a polynomial.

C: The state of the Turing Machine is unique for a particular step t. With s distinct states and S_t denoting the state of the Turing machine at time t, using our Boolean variable $S_{<k,t>}$, we can derive S_t as:

$$S_t = S_{<1,t>} \oplus S_{<2,t>} \oplus S_{<3,t>} \oplus \ldots\ldots\ldots \oplus S_{<s,t>}$$

(C1)

We know that the Turing Machine can go through at most $p(n)$ steps. Therefore, extending the above expression (C1) for every step, the constraint is expressed as follows:

$$C = S_0 \wedge S_1 \wedge S_2 \wedge S_3 \wedge \ldots\ldots\ldots\ldots S_{p(n)}$$

(C2)

Similar to the earlier constraints, the length of the above expression will be bounded by $s^2 p(n)$, which is clearly of $O(p(n))$.

D: Only the cell contents pointed by the head may change at every step.

This constraint means, at every transition from step t and $t+1$, the cell that may change is the one that is read by the head at step t. In other words, either the head is scanning cell i at time t or the value in cell i do not change between time t and $t+1$. The value at every other cell should remain unchanged. We can encode this constraint the following way:

$$c_{<i,j,t>} = c_{<i,j,t+1>} \vee H_{<i,t>}$$

Expanding the above for all cells, every step, and every possible symbol that the cell can have, we arrive at the following expression:

$$\text{D}= \prod_{i=1\, j=1\, t=0}^{i,t=p(n)\, j=m} (c_{<i,j,t+1>} \vee H_{<i,t>})$$

With j ranging from 1 through m, i ranging from 1 through $p(n)$, and t ranging from 0 through $p(n)$, the length of the above expression will be bounded by $mp(n)^2$, which is $O(p(n)^2)$, again a polynomial.

E: A change in the Turing Machine is specified through the transition relation δ. Let us dissect a specific transition configured part of δ. At step t, when the head is under cell i with value j and k being the Turing machine's state, then at step $t+1$, the following is expected to happen:

- The state can change from k to one of the s states, denoted by k_l.
- The value in the cell i can change from j to another value j_l.
- The Head of the Turing machine can move to a different cell, i.e., a step left or right, denoted by i_l.

$$\sum_l S_{<k_l,t+1>} \wedge c_{<i,j_l,t+1>} \wedge H_{<i_l,t+1>}$$

The Boolean OR in the above expression is required because the machine is an NTM, and there can be more than one target state at time t. The length of this expression is bound by the number of states s. Also, we would need to include the complement of the above condition to express our constraint fully, i.e., when the above expression is false, then at step t, either the head is not in the cell i, (or) the value in cell i is not j, (or) the state is not k. Adding this to the original equation, we get the following:

$$E = \sum_{i=1,t=0,j=1,k=1}^{i,t=p(n),j=m,k=s}$$

$$(\neg H_{<i,t>} \vee \neg S_{<1,t>} \vee \neg c_{<i,1,t>} \vee$$

$$\sum_{l} S_{<k_l,t+1>} \wedge c_{<i,j_l,t+1>} \wedge H_{<i_l,t+1>})$$

We can see that the length of the above expression is upper bounded by $smp(n)^2$, which is $O(p(n)^2)$.

F: The Turing Machine begins with the Initial State—q_1. We had assumed the initial state to be q_1, and we know that the length of the input string to be of length n. We can encode this constraint through the following expression:

$$F =$$

$$H_{<1,0>} \wedge S_{<1,0>} \wedge c_{<1,x,0>} \wedge c_{<2,x,0>} \cdot\cdot$$

$$\wedge c_{<n,x,0>} \wedge c_{<n+1,ƀ,0>} \wedge c_{<n+2,ƀ,0>} \cdots \wedge c_{<p(n),ƀ,0>}$$

The above expression captures the state of the Turing machine at time $t = 0$, which includes the following:

- The Head is at cell 1, which we can denote using $H_{<1,0>}$.
- The State of the Turing machine is q_1, which we can denote using $S_{<1,0>}$.
- The input string is from positions 1 through n, which we can denote using the following expression: $c_{<1,x,0>} \wedge c_{<2,x,0>} \cdot\cdot \wedge c_{<n,x,0>}$

  Here, x corresponds to one of the valid symbols from τ.
- The remainder cells, i.e., beyond n, are blank, which we can denote using the following expression. $c_{<n+1,ƀ,0>} \wedge c_{<n+2,ƀ,0>} \cdots \wedge c_{<p(n),ƀ,0>}$

Remember, blank is also considered part of τ.

We can see that this constraint's expression is $O(p(n))$.

G: The Turing Machine halts at the final state—q_2. Of all the constraints, this constraint has the most straightforward encoding, and it goes by the following, i.e., the state of the Turing machine at step $p(n)$ is q_2:

$$G = S_{<2,p(n)>}$$

We can see that this constraint is $O(1)$.

We have now seen that, of each of the seven constraints, the first constraint (A) is the most complex one whose encoding is $O(p(n)^3)$. But the good news is, $p(n)^3$ is a polynomial. By proving that the encoding of the seven constraints can happen in polynomial-time, we have proved that SAT is $NP-complete$.

9. INDEX

ABOUT THE AUTHOR

Ramaswami Mohandoss was born and raised in Chennai, India. Programming was the first love that pulled him into Computer Science during his teens. He is now a seasoned technologist with over two decades of Software Engineering experience. He has authored over twelve white papers in Data & AI and has filed two patents. In this book, he returns to his roots to explain the most important problem in theoretical Computer Science.

Printed in Great Britain
by Amazon

48856550R00106